May God ever bless you,
Luke Zimmer, ss.cc.

FATHER LUKE ZIMMER, SS.CC. was ordained a priest of the Congregation of the Sacred Hearts of Jesus and Mary on June 5, 1954. He has served as vocation director, associate pastor, seminary professor and superior. After working for several years in the Family Home Missions, he received permission from his superiors in 1971 to begin the actual work of the Apostolate of Christian Renewal which had been his desire since making his own personal Commitment some 26 years earlier. Archbishop Timothy Manning gave him permission to begin his work in the Archdiocese of Los Angeles.

The symbol of the Dove and Rainbow is taken from the Old Testament scene of the flood. Noah sent the Dove out and she brought back an olive branch, which is a sign of Peace. The Rainbow is a symbol of the promise of God not to destroy the world again by water. It is a sign of the Covenant He made with man. It is a symbol of renewal.

The picture of Jesus and Mary is used to show that the renewal of the spiritual life will come to the world through them. We are to go through Mary to Christ; with Christ to the Father in the Holy Spirit.

APOSTOLIC RENEWAL

Fr. Luke Zimmer, ss.cc.

alba house
DIVISION OF THE SOCIETY OF ST. PAUL
STATEN ISLAND, N.Y. 10314

Nihil Obstat:
Rev. Msgr. Patrick Dignan, Ph.D.

Imprimatur:
+John J. Ward, D.D., J.C.L.
Auxiliary Bishop of Los Angeles
Vicar General
Oct. 29, 1971

The Nihil Obstat and Imprimatur are a declaration that a book or pamphlet is considered to be free from doctrinal or moral error. It is not implied that those who have granted the Nihil Obstat and Imprimatur agree with the contents, opinions or statements expressed.

LIBRARY OF CONGRESS
CATALOGING IN PUBLICATION DATA

Zimmer, Luke B
  Apostolic renewal.

  1. Christian life—Catholic authors. 2. Catholic Church—Doctrinal and controversial works—Catholic authors. 3. Catholic Church—Prayer-books and devotions—English. I. Title.
BX2350.2.Z56   248'.48'2   73-5886
ISBN 0-8189-0275-2

With Permission:
Harold Whelan, SS.CC., Ph.D.
Provincial
June 27, 1972

Copyright 1973 by Luke B. Zimmer, SS.CC.

Designed, printed and bound in the United States of America by the Fathers and Brothers of the Society of St. Paul, 2187 Victory Boulevard, Staten Island, N. Y. 10314 as part of their communications apostolate.

Dedicated to
Pope John XXIII
And
Pope Paul VI

"Love one another, my dear children!
Seek rather what unites,
not what may separate you
From one another.
As I take leave, or better still,
As I say 'til we meet again'
Let me remind you of the
Most important things in life:
Our Blessed Savior Jesus; His good news; His church, truth and kindness.
I shall remember you all
And pray for you."
Last Testament of Pope John XXIII

"Just as with the teen-ager of the Gospel, Jesus Christ calls you to walk with Him: to offer your abilities, your efforts, your intelligence for the spread of His Kingdom—Jesus fed the multitudes with five loaves and two fishes and He knows how to use your contribution to the apostolate, small as it may be, to work wonders."
Pope John XXIII

"The Apostolate would lose its interior roots, its best forms, its highest ends—if the Apostle were not a man of Prayer."
Pope Paul VI

Permission obtained to use quotes from:

The Prophet by Kahlil Gibran, Alfred A Knopf, Inc. Publishers, New York. L.C. catalog number 53-9594

Meditations and Devotions by John Henry Newman, Templegate, Springfield, Ill.

Life and Holiness by Thomas Merton, Image Books, Herder & Herder, Inc. New York

Documents of Vatican II by Walter J. Abbott, S.J. Geoffrey Chapman Publishers 35 Red Lion Square London, W C I R 4 S G; And World Publishers, New York

Father Henri Systermans, SS. CC., Superior General of the Sacred Hearts Fathers presented Father Luke to His Holiness, Pope Paul VI in a private audience on December 17, 1969. His Holiness told Father Luke, *"I bless your work. I bless you and anyone who spreads this apostolate"*.

TABLE OF CONTENTS

FOREWORD 36

Section I

1. Life 14
2. Supernatural Life—Sharing in God's Life 22
3. The Christian Way 37
   a) The Blessed Virgin Mary, the Mother of Jesus Christ, the God-Man; The Mother of Men, and the Mother of the Church 37
   b) Jesus Christ, the Son of God; the God-Man, the Redeemer 42
   c) The Holy Spirit, the God of Love, Paraclete, Advocate, and Sanctifier 49
4. Living in the Presence of God 84
5. Prayer in Christian Renewal 96
6. Apostolic Works 131

Section II

7. Guidelines of the Apostolate of Christian Renewal 163
8. Preparation for Total Commitment 166
9. Ceremonies and Prayers 174

Section III

10. Daily Prayers 188

Section IV

11. Catalog 196

Foreword

A New Springtime

Shortly before Pope Pius XII died, he said that he envisioned the Church as entering upon a new dawn, a new springtime in which it would flourish and grow. Soon after, Pope John XXIII, by an impulse of Divine Providence, convoked an ecumenical council—Vatican Council II.

> As regards the initiative for the great event which gathers us here, it will suffice to repeat as historical documentation our personal account of the first sudden bringing up in our heart and lips of the simple words, "Ecumenical Council." We uttered these words in the presence of the Sacred College of Cardinals on that memorable January 25, 1959, the feast of the Conversion of St. Paul, in the basilica dedicated to him. It was completely unexpected, like a flash of heavenly light, shedding sweetness in eyes and hearts. And at the same time it gave rise to a great fervor throughout the world in expectation of the holding of the Council. (Pope John XXIII's opening speech at Vatican Council II.)

Call to Ponder Heavenly Things

It was the hope of Pope John XXIII that the Vatican Council II would bring men, families, and people to really turn their minds to heavenly things.

> Illuminated by the light of this Council, the Church—we confidently trust—will become greater in spiritual riches and, gaining the strength of new energies therefrom, she will look to the future without fear. In fact, by bringing herself up to date where required, and by wise organization of mutual cooperation, the Church will make men, families, and peoples really turn their minds to heavenly things. (*Ibid.*)

Duty of Vatican Council II—Uphold & Foster Truth

In another part of his speech, Pope John XXIII tells us the principal duty of the Council: The defense and advancement of truth. It would be well to quote the entire passage.

The greatest concern of the Ecumenical Council is this: that the sacred deposit of Christian doctrine should be guarded and taught more efficaciously. That doctrine embraces the whole of man, composed as he is of body and soul. And, since he is a pilgrim on this earth, it commands him to tend always toward heaven.

This demonstrates how our mortal life is to be ordered in such a way as to fulfill our duties as citizens of earth and of heaven, and thus to attain the aim of life as established by God. That is, all men, whether taken singly or as united in society, today have the duty of tending ceaselessly duing their lifetime toward the attainment of heavenly things and to use, for this purpose only, the earthly goods, the employment of which must not prejudice their eternal happiness.

The Lord has said: 'Seek first the Kingdom of God and His justice' (Mt. 6:33). The word 'first' expresses the direction in which our thoughts and energies must move. We must not, however, neglect the other words of this exhortation of our Lord, namely: 'And all these things shall be given you besides' (ibid.). In reality, there always have been in the Church, and there are still today, those who, while seeking the practice of evangelical perfection with all their might, do not fail to make themselves useful to society. Indeed, it is from their constant example of life and their charitable undertakings that all that is highest and noblest in human society takes its strength and growth.

In order, however, that this doctrine may influence the numerous fields of human activity, with reference to individuals, to families, and to social life, it is necessary first of all that the Church should never depart from the sacred patrimony of truth received from the Fathers. But at the same time she must ever look to the present, to the new conditions and new forms of life introduced into the modern world which have opened new avenues to the Catholic apostolate.

For this reason, the Church has not watched inertly the marvelous progress of the discoveries of human genius, and has not been backward in evaluating them rightly. But, while following these developments, she does not neglect to admonish men so that, over and above sense-perceived things—they may raise their eyes to God, the Source of all wisdom and all beauty. And may they never forget the most serious command: 'The Lord thy God shalt thou worship, and Him alone shalt thou serve' (Mt. 4:10; Lk. 4:8), so that it may not happen that the fleeting fascination of visible things should impede true progress.

The manner in which sacred doctrine is spread, this having been established, it becomes clear how much is expected for the Council in regard to doctrine. That is, the Twenty-first Ecumenical Council, which will draw upon the effective and important wealth of juridical, liturgical, apostolic, and administrative experiences, wishes to transmit the doctrine, pure and integral, without any attenuation or distortion, which throughout twenty centuries, notwithstanding difficulties and contrasts, has become the common patrimony of men. It is a patrimony not well received by all, but always a rich treasure available to men of good will.

Our duty is not only to guard this precious treasure, as if we were concerned only with antiquity, but to dedicate ourselves with an earnest will and without fear to that work which our era demands of us, pursuing thus the path which the Church has followed for twenty centuries.

The salient point of this Council is not, therefore, a discussion on one article or another of the fundamental doctrines of the Church which has repeatedly been taught by the Fathers and by ancient and modern theologians, and which is presumed to be well known and familiar to all.

For this a Council was not necessary. But from the renewed, serene, and tranquil adherence to all the teachings of the Church, in its entirety and preciseness, as it still shines forth in the Acts of the Council of Trent and the First Vatican Council, the Christian, Catholic, and apostolic spirit of the whole world expects a step forward to a doctrinal penetration, and a formation of consciousness in faithful and perfect conformity to the authentic doctrine, which, however, should be studied and expounded through the methods of research and through the literary forms of modern thought. The substance of the ancient doctrine of the deposit of faith is one thing, and the way in which it is presented is another. And it is the latter that must be taken into great consideration with patience if necessary, everything being measured in the forms and proportions of a magisterium which is predominantly pastoral in character.

Signs of The Times

From the words of Pope John XXIII, we can clearly see that he was concerned that the truths of the Church be protected, upheld, and fostered. We also see that he urged the Church to bring its message to the modern world. Pope John knew the "Signs of the times," that there is a crisis of faith in the modern world. Yet, we see that he had hope and confidence for a bright future. We see this from the words he used in his apostolic constitution *Humanae Salutis* dated December 25, 1961, when he convoked the Second Vatican Council for sometime in 1962.

Today the Church is witnessing a crisis under way within society. While humanity is on the edge of a new era, tasks of immense gravity and amplitude await the Church, as in the most tragic periods of its history. It is a question in fact of bringing the modern world into contact with the vivifying and perennial energies of the Gospel, a world which exalts itself with its conquests in the technical and scientific fields, but which brings also the consequences of a temporal order which some have wished to reorganize excluding God. This is why modern society is earmarked by a great material progress to which there is not a corresponding advance in the moral field.

Hence there is a weakening in the aspiration toward the values of the spirit. Hence an urge for the almost exclusive search for earthly pleasures, which progressive technology places with such ease within the reach of all. And hence there is a completely new and disconcerting fact: the existence of a militant atheism which is active on a world level.

These painful considerations are a reminder of the duty to be vigilant and to keep the sense of responsibility awake. Distrustful souls see only darkness burdening the face of the earth. We, instead, like to reaffirm all our confidence in our Savior, Who has not left the world which He redeemed.

Indeed, we make ours the recommendation of Jesus that one should know how to distinguish the 'signs of the times' (Mt. 16:4), and we seem to see now, in the midst of so much darkness, a few indications which augur well for the fate of the Church and of humanity.

The bloody wars that have followed one on the other in our times, the spiritual ruins caused by many ideologies, and the fruits of so many bitter experiences have not been without useful teachings. Scientific progress itself, which gave man the possibility of creating catastrophic instruments for his destruction, has raised questions. It has obliged human beings to become thoughtful, more conscious of their own limitations, desirous of peace, and attentive to the importance of spiritual values. And it has accelerated that progress of closer collaboration and of mutual integration towards which, even though in the midst of a thousand uncertainties, the human family seems to be moving. And this facilitates, no doubt, the apostolate of the Church, since many people who did not realize the importance of its mission in the past are, taught by experience, today more disposed to welcome its warnings.

Then, if we turn our attention to the Church, we see that it has not remained a lifeless spectator in the face of these events, but has followed step by step the evolution of peoples, scientific progress, and social revolution. It has opposed decisively the materialistic ideologies which deny faith. Lastly, it has witnessed the rise and growth of the immense energies of the apostolate of prayer, of action in all fields. It has seen the emergence of a clergy constantly better equipped in learning and virtue for its mission; and of a laity which has become ever more conscious of its responsibilities within the bosom of the Church, and, in a special way, of its duty to collaborate with the Church hierarchy.

To this should be added the immense suffering of entire Christian communities, through which a multitude of admirable bishops, priests and laymen seal their adherence to the faith, bearing persecutions of all kinds and revealing forms of heroism which certainly equal those of the most glorious periods of the Church.

Thus, though the world may appear profoundly changed, the Christian community is also in great part transformed and renewed. It has therefore strengthened itself socially in unity; it has been reinvigorated intellectually; it has been interiorly purified and thus ready for trial.

Trials

Indeed, the trials have come to the Church since the closing of Vatican Council II. It seems that no doctrine of faith and morals has been untouched. Doubts, criticism, and even rejection of the doctrines of the Church have been the order of the day. The bark of Peter is being threatened by the upsurging of these waves. Yet, we must hope and have courage because Christ is present within the Church, even though He may seem to be asleep. Let our faith in the Church be strong so that we will not receive the rebuke of Christ, "Oh, you of little faith" (cf. Mk. 4:35-40; Mt. 8: 23-27). We must learn to keep our eyes on Christ and we will not falter, lose heart, and sink as Peter did when he went to meet Christ walking on the water (Cf. Mt. 14: 22-33). In that passage Christ rebuked Peter too: "Oh, you of little faith, why do you doubt?"

Truth Will Prevail

We know that the truth of the Lord will remain forever, and that error will never prevail. Rather, it will disappear, and the clouds of doubt, criticism, and rejection will give way to a brighter day.

What should our attitude be toward those who teach falsehood and lead the faithful astray? Our attitude should be one of mercy and charity so that they may be led back to Christ, Who is the way, the truth, and the life. How will one know if someone is teaching falsehood? Christ told us, "By their fruits we shall know them" (cf. Mt. 7: 15-20).

> At the onset of the Second Vatican Council, it is evident, as always, that the truth of the Lord will remain forever. We see, in fact, as one age succeeds another, that the opinions of men follow one another and exclude each other. And often errors vanish as they arise, like fog before the sun.
>
> The Church has always opposed these errors. Frequently she has condemned them with the greatest severity. Nowadays, however, the

Spouse of Christ prefers to make use of the medicine of mercy rather than that of severity. She considers that she meets the needs of the present day by demonstrating the validity of her teaching rather than by condemnations. Not, certainly, that there is a lack of fallacious teaching, opinions, and dangerous concepts to be guarded against and dissipated. But these are so obviously in contrast with the right norm of honesty, and have produced such lethal fruits, that by now it would seem that men of themselves are inclined to condemn them, particularly those ways of life which displease God and His law or place excessive confidence in technical progress and a well-being based exclusively on the comforts of life. They are ever more deeply convinced of the paramount dignity of the human person and of his perfections, as well as of the duties which that implies. Even more important, experience has taught men that violence inflicted on others, the might of arms, and political domination are of no help at all in finding a happy solution to the grave problems which afflict them.

That being so, the Catholic Church, raising the torch of religious truth by means of the Ecumenical Council, desires to show herself to be the loving mother of all, benign, patient, full of mercy and goodness toward the brethren who are separated from her. To mankind, oppressed by so many difficulties, the Church says, as Peter said to the poor who begged alms from him: 'I have neither gold or silver, but what I have I give you; in the name of Jesus Christ of Nazareth, rise and walk' (Acts 3:6). In other words, the Church does not offer to the men of today riches that pass, nor does she promise them a merely earthly happiness. But she distributes to them the goods of divine grace which, raising men to the dignity of sons of God, are the most efficacious safeguards and aids toward a more human life. She opens the fountain of her life-giving doctrine which allows men, enlightened by the light of Christ, to understand well what they really are, what their lofty dignity and their purpose are, and, finally through her children, she spreads everywhere the fullness of Christian charity, than which nothing is more effective in eradicating the seeds of discord, nothing more efficacious in promoting concord, just peace, and the brotherly unity of all.

(*Pope John XXIII's opening speech at Vatican Council II*)

Magna Carta of The Church

The documents of Vatican Council II should be for us the Magna Carta of the Church. In the documents, we find the directives and guidelines for making the Church relevant in the modern world. If we read the documents we will see that the Holy Father and the Church have been faithfully carrying out the directives for updating and renewal. It would be well for us to keep our ears and mind open to the words and teachings of our Holy Father, the Vicar of Christ. Christ speaks to us through him, and Pope Paul VI has been fulfilling his office of Shepherd of the faithful in an admirable way. He is not swayed by public opinion, but forcefully and constantly proclaims the teachings of Christ. If we listen to him, keep an open mind, and not harden our hearts, we will never be led astray. Our faith will always be vibrant and strong.

Christ said that He is the vine and we are the branches and if we remain in Him we will bear much fruit. I like to think of the Church as a tree with each member as a branch, or a twig, or a leaf. The sap of the tree circulates and penetrates each branch, twig, or leaf. The sap in the Church is the life of Christ which circulates through His Church into the branches, twigs, and leaves through the life-giving Sacraments. The tree could also represent the doctrines of the Church, and the branches, twigs, and leaves the means by which these doctrines are extended out for the health and beauty of the Church.

Therefore we have a twofold dimension in the Church—the doctrine and the manner in which it is taught and practiced, we have Christ and His members. The doctrines of the Church cannot change because they are the truths taught by Christ Himself, but the manner of teaching them and carrying them out in practice can change and has changed down through the centuries, but more rapidly during the past few years.

Vatican Council II has pruned the tree, getting rid of what was dead, or what would hinder the health of the Church and its members. It has grafted on new methods, new ways of carrying out the doctrines, new forms of worship in the Church. Thus, the Church ever remains the same, but with new dimensions, just as a tree with a new graft remains the same but has new dimensions. Only in this way can we say that the Church and the tree have changed.

The grafting of the tree is done in the springtime, and soon we see the graft become a part of the tree itself. In springtime the dead twigs and branches are pruned away so that the tree can begin the life-giving process of blossoming and producing fruit. The dead leaves fall off because they have withered and dried up. As the spring advances we see the new leaves appear, the blossoms come forth, and the beauty of the tree unfolds before our eyes.

True Springtime—Union With Christ

Like the tree, the grafting of the Church has taken place, the dead branches have been removed, and the leaves have fallen. Let us hope that the true springtime of the Church is rapidly approaching as envisioned by Pope Pius XII. Now is the time to see the tree come alive. Soon we may see the Church putting forth new buds and new leaves, and the branches that seem to be dead become vigorous with life. May the blossoms be numerous and the fruit plentiful. This is the process that seems to be taking place in the Church today.

It would be well to read and meditate upon the fifteenth chapter of St. John's Gospel in which he speaks of union with Christ. Union with Christ is so important for each one of us if we wish to remain faithful to His teachings and to His Church; if we wish to remain in His love. Christ came to us from His Father, born of the ever blessed Virgin Mary through the power of the Holy Spirit. Thus we should go back to the Father with Christ, through Mary, in the Holy Spirit.

All true devotion to the Blessed Virgin Mary leads us to Christ, and that is why the Apostolate of Christian Renewal has a special devotion to Mary. She will lead us to Him in a simple and rapid way. Our love for Christ will increase as our devotion to Mary grows, and when we love Christ He will bring us to the Father. Then, as He said, the Father and Christ will come to dwell within us. Then, He will ask the Father to send us the Holy Spirit. We become aware of the presence of the Triune God within us, and we freely accept the action of the Holy Spirit, who forms Christ in us so that we become Christlike—we put on the Lord Jesus Christ. We all know that we receive the indwelling of the Triune God at our baptism, but now we actually become aware of this presence. The life of God increases and grows from day to day, from month to month, from year to year and throughout our life, until we are ready to go home to dwell with God for all eternity.

Holiness—Being A Whole Christian

This is the life of holiness that Vatican Council II is calling each one of us to live. This is what we hope to accomplish by having established the Apostolate of Christian Renewal. It is a life of love, of prayer, of service to others. It is to be a whole Christian. It is not meant to be pietistical; rather it is meant to be a complete integrated Christian life, where love rather than fear, where the positive rather than the negative is stressed. We are to live with the freedom of the Children of God, putting the Beatitudes of Our Lord into effect. We do this by developing our interior spiritual life and by our service to others. We do this in the Church, with the Church, and through the Church. Therefore, we gladly accept the institutional Church established by Christ.

Individual Freedom & Responsibility

It was the intention of Vatican Council II to place more responsibility upon the individual in developing his spiritual life, in building the community—the Kingdom of God. That is why many things have been changed in the Church. The changes have caused pain, confusion, and even open rebellion. However, they should help each one of us to become a better Christian, if only we would be open and accept our responsibility to do our part.

Certain rules and regulations have been abrogated and each one is left to develop his own mode of action. Because of this, some people feel lost and are floundering, trying to feel their way. Some rules and regulations can never be changed because they are from God. We have to learn to make the proper distinctions, upholding God's rules and regulations, while being free in the areas in which the Church has directed we could be. But if we truly loved God, and our neighbor, we would observe all the rules and regulations of the Church and of God. We would not even think of them because our actions and thoughts would always be upright. Then, we would never feel burdened or oppressed by rules, laws, or commandments. We would truly be free and live our commitment with conviction, because we want to do what God wishes.

I wish to establish the Apostolate of Christian Renewal with the same spirit of freedom and responsibility granted to the People of God by Vatican Council II. Therefore, I do not intend to have set rules and regulations in regard to prayer or service to others. Rather, I wish to give guidelines and suggestions which are not binding in conscience.

I hope that each one who makes the Commitment to Jesus Christ through Mary will have a deep conviction in what he or she is doing. That he or she will develop a program of prayer and service. This should be worked out with a spiritual director. Each one could act as an individual, but I would prefer that a group be formed in each parish, diocese, and civic community so that not only the individual will benefit, but that through united action and prayer, the whole community will be benefited. This group should work under the direction of the pastor in a parish, under the bishop in a diocese, and under civic leaders in a civic community. Thus we would have a variety of ways in which the Apostolate could develop. Each area would be free to implement the Apostolate in the way that would be the most effective in achieving its goal.

I wish to establish the Apostolate of Christian Renewal as a pious union so that there will be a bond of unity between everyone who makes his or her Commitment to Jesus Christ through Mary.

I have thought about establishing this Apostolate over a period of twenty-five years; therefore it is not the result of hasty decision or action. I have prayed much and suffered, too, over these many years, wondering what God really wishes in regard to the Apostolate. It seems to me that God wishes that the Apostolate of Christian Renewal be started now, and it is my prayer that it will contribute to bringing about the springtime of the Church; that it will produce love, joy, and happiness in the lives of each member, in the groups formed, and in the communities in which the Apostolate is established.

May God give you the generosity to make your Commitment —your covenant with Him. May God bless you and may He give you abundant life!

Section One
LIFE

When our astronauts landed on the moon they described it as a very desolate place because, no matter where they looked, they saw no form of life. There was not even a cactus like those found in the desert on earth. Later, scientists discovered that there was not even a live germ on the moon. It is indeed a desolate place, without life, barren.

We often speak of the desert as a barren and desolate place, because there is little or no life present. We can travel for miles and see nothing but dry sand, sand dust blown about by the wind. We might see a cactus here and there, and some of them have real beauty, but little water or anything that can sustain life is to be found there. Yet, with irrigation, even the desert can be changed into a beautiful place.

What a contrast to the desert and the moon is a place teeming with flowers, trees, and natural beauty! Most of us have experienced the beauty of nature, and many of us have taken it all for granted, but there are times when all of us are deeply impressed with the panoramic view before us. It could be a mountain, a canyon, the ocean, a valley, a garden, a park, or a forest. It is then we begin to realize what life is and our heart fills with the joy of living. The wonder of it all moves us in the depths of our being and gradually our thoughts take on a new dimension. We begin to wonder where it all came from. Surely it had a beginning. Even if we believe in evolution, we still must ask, how did it all begin? Our minds are elevated to contemplate a higher power who made all this possible and who sustains everything in being. We soon become aware of the presence of God around us. Therefore, in contemplating nature and its beauty we can communicate with our God, because nature itself cries out—There is a God!

The astronauts, upon their return, said that they were glad to be back on "good earth," and we can readily agree. Yet, all the glory and beauty of the good earth of itself remains only natural.

Plant Life

The small seed contains within its shell the power to nurture the flower, the tree, the plant, which will bring beauty to the world. Yet, even in the lowest form of life the mystery of death seems to play a part. The seed must be planted in the earth for the plant to grow. The key to the process of life is that the seed has to die in order to give life to the plant. In dying, the seed takes nourishment from the ground and transmits it to the growing plant.

If the seed is planted in shallow ground, it will spring up quickly, but without deep roots that tap water and minerals from the earth, the plant will wither from the sun and the wind and collapse without roots. If this same seed is planted in too wet or too rich soil, all the strength will go into the first growth and leave nothing for the blossoms. Only the ideal soil is safe for the proper growth of the seed and the dying process and the rebirth.

We know that even this plant can be destroyed because of disease from within and its enemies from without. That is why a caretaker is necessary to see that the plant develops and matures and bears fruit. Even the plant cannot develop properly on its own. It requires the help of other beings.

Even so, the yearly cycle of plant life is one of the marvels of the world.

Animal Life

We are blessed on earth to have another higher form of being, and that is animal life. Just like the plant, the animal has power to mature and reproduce. Unlike the plant, the animal is able to move by its own power from place to place. It is able to express feelings of pain, sadness, joy and companionship. It, too, depends on other beings for its survival. The animals of the jungle follow the rule of "survival of the fittest," while domestic animals are more dependent on man. When we see animals we cannot help but admire their beauty and majesty. Again our minds are elevated to a higher power who made them and sustains them in being. Like the natural beauty of the plant, the animal often leads us to contemplation of God.

Human Life

The highest form of being on earth is man. Who is man? This question has plagued us for centuries, but at no time in history has the individual human being sought so desperately for the truth about himself and the world in which he lives. This seems to be the lot of the modern world, that the question of identity, of understanding one's real nature, is not just a personal quest. Nations are undergoing the same searching, the same yearning for a glimpse of truth. Modern man and the world with him is searching for identity.

When we contemplate man, we see that like the plants he can mature and reproduce; like the animals he can express feelings of pain, sadness, joy, and companionship. He has power to move from one place to another. But unlike the plant or animal he can think, express ideas, and put these ideas into action. Plants have processes that keep them functioning. Animals have instincts and senses. Man has these too, but man's soul is different from the souls of plants or brute animals. Man has reason and free will, the tools God gave him to take dominion over the world. God created all things in the world and gave them to man for his use so that he could give glory to God. Therefore, all things on earth are related to man as their center and crown.

> What is man that you are mindful of him or the son of man that you visited him? You have made him a little less than the angels, you have crowned him with glory and honor: You have set him over the works of your hands, you have subjected all things under his feet (Ps. 8: 5-6).

Man's Supernatural Life

Man's soul is immortal. We know this from Divine Revelation.

It is something we can accept on faith, and yet it is proved within ourselves. We can truly believe that our souls are immortal because all our acts of intelligence and free will (thinking, praying, choosing good or evil) are spiritual acts, not confined to the flesh or rooted in our bodies. Our souls are spiritual, not dependent upon matter and not subject to death and decay. If scientists today understand that matter cannot totally disappear, however minute the particle, how can the soul of man, of a far higher order in creation, be thought to suffer extinction?

Man has mind and free will. He can reflect, plan ahead for the future, reason out problems that come into his life, and make judgments about others and about situations. He longs for true happiness, a happiness not marred with the passage of time or with illness. This longing is a cross and vexation, but all men have it in common. Things created beneath us cannot satisfy us, no matter how many objects we own. People, our equals in creation, cannot always satisfy us either, for we see them change and move away from us. We love and share our lives with others, but we realize that we are still alone, as we were born and as we shall die. Only God can give us the joy we seek. He created our souls for Himself. That is why our hearts are restless until they rest in Him. Man has the power to know the truth, to know goodness; even to grasp the source of all truth, or all goodness, God Himself. Only man can dream of eternity with God.

Ancient civilizations recognized eternal life and the eternal qualities of the soul. Even pagan civilizations that had no Divine Revelation had their abodes for the dead. Egypt made a cult out of death. Life on earth was to be understood as a preparation for the judgment halls, in which the goddess Maat weighed the hearts of Egyptians to see if they were heavy enough with love.

Evolution?

Modern man can no longer accept vague legends or strange cults. He attempts to explain his existence by the theory of evolution, and modern atheists try to explain away man's longing for immortality. To them, man is just a higher form of animal that has evolved from the ape. There is a constant search to find the missing link which would prove this theory. Yet it remains just a theory; it is not a scientifically proven fact.

Even if science could prove that man evolved from the ape we would still believe that God created the soul of man. We know that man is a composite—he has a body and soul, and this is what makes him a complete human person. Man is not just a higher form of animal composed of a body, nor does man just have a soul. We believe that man's soul is immortal and that it will never cease to exist. But to be a whole human person the body must be reunited to the soul. We believe this will happen after the resurrection. For this reason, we have to work for the salvation of the whole person, and not just the salvation of the soul.

Polygenesis

Modern man is also talking about the theory of polygenesis, but this theory poses some unresolved difficulties for Catholics because we believe that God created male and female, that is Adam and Eve, as the first parents of the human race. We believe that all men descended from them, and not from multiple parents. From the beginning, "male and female He created them" (Gen. 1: 27).

Reincarnation, Or Creation Of Man's Soul?

Many believe in reincarnation, but that, too, like evolution and polygenesis, remains just a theory—a supposition. It is not a scientifically proven fact. Modern psychologists and psychiatrists tell us that the theory of reincarnation is questionable because what appears to be knowledge of a former life is just sense impressions made upon our subconscious mind in our early present life.

We do not believe in reincarnation. It is true that we always existed, in the mind of God. With God there is no past or future, only an eternal now. *There was never a time that God did not think of us.* What a powerful concept this is—we existed from all eternity in the mind of God! We believe that man and woman become co-creators with God in bringing a human person into existence. Man supplies the body and God creates the soul. We believe that this happens at the moment of our conception. We also believe that our soul is made in the image and likeness of God. God Himself declared it.

> Let us make mankind in our image and likeness; and let them have dominion over the fish of the sea, the birds of the air, the cattle, over all the wild animals and every creature that crawls on the earth (Gen. 1:26).

What does it mean to be made in His image and likeness? It means that we have a spiritual soul with faculties of intellect and free will. We also have other spiritual powers which are God-like. It is not in our body that we have a likeness to God, or are made in His image. Yet, the body is necessary for us to be a complete human person.

Born Equal before God

Everyone is born equal in the eyes of God, whether we are rich or poor, sick or healthy, white or black, red or yellow, or brown. With God there is no distinction, since we are all made in His image and likeness.

> There is neither Jew nor Greek; there is neither slave nor freeman; there is neither male nor female. For you are all one in Christ Jesus (Gal. 3:28).

We are equal, too, in the sense that we are all children of God. God is our Father so we do belong to the same family — God's family. We are the People of God. We are brothers and sisters to each other. This, too, is a wonderful concept. Just think about it—everyone in the world is my brother or sister because God is our Father. If we really believed this and acted upon it, what a different world we would have.

Each Person is Unique

We know from experience that men are not equal in any other way, since each one has different qualities and talents. Each person is unique and has his own mission in the plan of God. Each person is important and precious in the sight of God. However, no one can carry out his mission alone. Man is not an island, but a social being. Unless he relates to others, he can never develop or achieve his potential. Therefore, he needs the help of others, and mainly the help of God, to work out his salvation.

Sharing In God's Life And Love

We may wonder what God's plan for us is and why He bothered even to create us. The only answer is His immeasurable love. Love and goodness is diffusive of itself. The one who loves wishes to share with others; to give love, goodness, happiness, and joy. Thus God created us so that we may have life and enjoy its abundance. Nor did God wish us to have these things for an earthly life alone. He wished to share His life, love, and happiness with us, and all of these are eternal.

God gave the tremendous gift of supernatural life to our first parents, Adam and Eve, but He gave them the gift of free will so that they could either live this supernatural life or reject it. We know that they chose to reject this gift, and that is how original sin came into the world. We are all affected by this sin because our human nature was wounded—our intellect was darkened and our will weakened.

Yet God's love for man could not be stifled, nor did He abandon him. He promised to send a Redeemer, the Messiah, so that this supernatural life could be restored. We believe that God the Father did send the Messiah, the Redeemer, in the person of Jesus Christ, the God-man. He came into the world to do His Father's will so that we could again share in the supernatural life.

This supernatural life is sharing in the very life of God Himself. A man knowing his own personal worth in the eyes of his Creator, understands, suddenly and joyously, that he was called to life on this earth and to infinite happiness in eternity. This interior supernatural life can grow, increase, mature and develop. Thus we can become Godlike even while on earth. It is the interior growth in the spiritual life that is necessary. This is the renewal that Vatican Council II is talking about. This is what we mean by Christian renewal. In other words, Christian, be aware of your great dignity as a person—as a child of God—as a member of His family.

SUPERNATURAL LIFE --
SHARING IN GOD'S LIFE!

One night Nicodemus came to Jesus to talk with Him because he realized that Jesus was a teacher come from God. Jesus told him, "I solemnly assure you, no one can see the reign of God unless he be begotten from above" (John 3:3). Nicodemus said, "How can a man be born again once he is old?" (John 3:4). Jesus replied: "I solemnly assure you, no one can enter into God's kingdom without being begotten of water and Spirit" (John 3:4). It is through baptism that we are given a share in God's life and we are initiated into God's family.

After Christ rose from the dead, He commissioned the Apostles to preach the Gospel to the whole world and to baptize all who believed.

> Full authority has been given to me both in heaven and on earth; go, therefore, and make disciples of all the nations. Baptize them in the name of the Father, and of the Son, and of the Holy Spirit. Teach them to carry out everything I have commanded you. And know that I am with you always, until the end of the World. (Mt. 28: 18-20)

Through baptism we receive a new dimension in our existence. We are elevated to a new form of life—to supernatural life. Through the sacrament of rebirth we become members of God's family; we have God the Father as our Father, and Christ as our Brother. The Triune God—the Father, Son, and Holy Spirit—come and dwell within us so that in all truth we can say, "the Kingdom of God is within us." We are given the gifts of faith, hope, and charity; the gifts of temperance, fortitude, prudence, and justice. We are also given the gifts of the Holy Spirit: Wisdom, knowledge, understanding, counsel, fortitude, piety, and fear of the Lord. However, these gifts are given to us only in an embryonic stage, and they are to be developed throughout our life. Baptism takes away original sin, and all actual personal sins, and all the punishment due to them. Baptism makes the individual person a member of the Church and a child of God. Baptism imprints an indelible sign or character on the soul. This character marks us as Christians, and cannot be removed by anything, even mortal sin. "For all you who have been baptized into Christ have put on Christ" (Gal. 3:27). Through baptism we are also made priests, prophets and kings. This is our heritage as baptized children of God.

Because we were baptized when we were small babies, many of us do not realize the tremendous happening that took place in our very being. We do not appreciate the dignity that was given to us as persons. It is a fact that many never come to this realization and go through life without grasping its meaning or purpose. Some do realize what was given to them at baptism, but since this is just an intellectual awareness, little or nothing is done to develop their spiritual life. It seems that only a few realize what life is all about, what it means to be a Christian. They are strong in their convictions and they try to develop their interior spiritual life.

A Mad Man, Or A Saint!

We always stand in awe in the presence of a newly baptized child. Why? Because a child is so lovable and loving; he is innocent and pure. Yet we often wonder, what will this child become? We all know that a child can become a sinner or a saint; become Godlike or a demon; be loving or filled with hate. It makes us realize that, *"Nothing happens on the face of the earth that has not already taken place within one human soul."* This statement has a profound and terrible significance for the modern world, a world that has at last understood the hideous consequences of madness and hatred born in one human soul and organized into agony for millions of others. The ruins of World War II, the present condition of countries enslaved by ideologies, the agony of Asia—all testify to the ringing truth of the power of one human being to influence thousands or millions for good or evil.

The annals of history add considerable significance to the statement when we remember an Adolph Hitler or a Francis of Assisi emerging from the chaos of their eras to straddle the world; terror and murder on one hand and consuming love that calls all men together on the other. Contrast these two historical figures and recognize the important roles they played for their own ages and for generations yet to come upon the earth.

Risk Of Life—How We Use Our Free Will

Meditate often on that statement—"*Nothing happens on the face of the earth that has not already taken place within one human soul.*" Why? Because this is the risk of life, and God took this risk when He gave everyone a free will. God will never interfere with anyone's free will. We all have the choice to follow Christ and do good or to reject Him and do evil. God, more than anyone else, treats us as persons. He respects us as persons and lets us enjoy our freedom. Neither is God a doting Father. His gifts are always there if we but accept them, but God leaves us free to use these gifts for His glory, for the development of our supernatural life, or to misuse them and abandon Him entirely. God never abandons us, nor leaves us orphans, unless we freely abandon Him. It is always a tragedy when anyone rejects God, or misuses His gifts, or fails to use these gifts to grow and mature in the supernatural life.

Importance of Good Home Life

The Christian, like the seeds which Christ spoke of in His parable, must be planted in truth and in secure goodness. Modern families, outside of those who understand the need for discipline and for holy example, often fail their children. The parents have given up any idea of dedication to Christian living and are engrossed in the daily pace of making money and winning friends. Modern youth especially see the hypocrisy of such an outlook on life, and they rebel against it and against the parents who practice it. Children are quite capable of seeing the emptiness and anxiety in their homes; they live with anger and cruelty and even hatred. Whatever gifts of God come to them wither because the soil is shallow—the home is agony for them, and the parents are like cruel winds that bite and maul them to pieces.

The opposite is true, of course. Those children blessed with good parents, with deep-rooted love in the home, with genuine understanding and affection, are able to absorb the example of charity and peace. Understanding love is something natural, within the reach of every human being. Such children, above all others, stand the chance of becoming more than beginners in the spiritual life. They develop a genuine horror of sin, because they realize that sin is death to their supernatural life, and even to the human personality. These children begin to pray and to live a life of intimacy with God. This sounds difficult in our day and age, but it requires no more than placing one's hand in His, and whispering our love in the quiet times of prayer. From it comes the courage to stand firm and do His Will even in the face of inconvenience, ridicule, or pain.

Die To Self—Transformed To Reflect Divine Love

Like the seed, the Christian has to die to himself in order that his supernatural life might increase. What does this involve? It is a simple surrendering, a simple act of love that does not belittle the Christian or injure him but rather frees him for the graces that God would give. The Christian understands that he has little to offer anyone, and he begs graces and the touch of God so that he will be transformed slowly, gently, into the reflection of Divine love. It means not wanting what will benefit one's own self, but knowing that the Will of God will bring peace and joy to all and that this Divine Will must be the entire occupation of the individual. It means understanding that God created each human being for Himself, so that one learns to love all human beings, not clinging to those who can give him pleasure or happiness, but helping everyone who stands in equality before the Creator.

False Love, Or True Love?

What is love in our world today? In the motion pictures, love has been presented in a very dehumanized way. Love in the movies is a physical, one dimensional act, a moment's snatching of pleasure without joy, without laughter, without the beauty of the spirit in its embrace. Our children see this love and they are frightened, because it is a brutal act, an ugly game that offers them no hope or refreshment.

Love has also been drained of its power by shallow slogans and abstract generalizations. Although we certainly must love and sympathize with the suffering people around the world, to be a truly loving human being we must genuinely commit ourselves and our energies to service of the people we actually come in contact with.

Kahlil Gibran, the Arabic poet who is very popular today, tried to tell the people of every age what to expect from love when he said:

> When love beckons to you follow him,
> Though his ways are hard and steep.
> And when his wings enfold you, yield to him
> Though the sword hidden among his pinions may wound you.
> And when he speaks to you believe him,
> Though his voice may shatter your dreams
>   as the north wind lays waste the garden.
> For even as love crowns you, so shall he crucify you.
> Even as he is for your growth so he is for your pruning....
> When you love you should not say, 'God is in my heart'
>   but rather, 'I am in the heart of God!

We all understand the words of this poet. We may not know why he uses the particular phrases he does or why they sing to us, but we know what he means because we have lived that way ourselves, sometimes without meaning to live at all. If we are parents, we know what it is to love without asking in return, to share without knowing if there will be anything left for us, to correct and to rule without asking that the children understand us now.

If we have loved other people, we know what it is to be wounded by love. Our dreams, built so easily upon the smile of another, may have been shattered, the way the north wind shatters the poet's garden. We understand the poet, for he speaks as a human being to us all, who have experiences very much in common.

True Love!

Still, living the life of love is more than poetic phrases or bright images. To live the life of love commanded by Christ is to transport our very beings into conflicts and agonies and suffering. We need strength beyond poetic songs. We need to understand what love is in God's Will for us all.

St. Paul offers us the classic example of what love is when he describes it for those who would follow Christ's commands. Look at this essay on charity and translate the word charity into love so that you can understand what it truly means, today as yesterday.

> If I should speak with the tongues of men and angels, but do not have charity (love) I have become as sounding brass or a tinkling cymbal. And if I have all prophecy and know all mysteries and all knowledge, and if I have all faith so as to remove mountains, yet do not have charity (love), I am nothing. And if I distribute all my goods to feed the poor and if I deliver my body to be burned, yet do not have charity (love), it profits me nothing.
>
> Love is patient, is kind; love does not envy, is not pretentious, is not puffed up, is not ambitious, is not self-seeking, is not provoked; thinks no evil, does not rejoice over wickedness, but rejoices with the truth; bears all things, believes all things, hopes all things, endures all things.
>
> Love never fails, whereas prophecies will disappear, and tongues will cease and knowledge will be destroyed ... So there abide faith, hope and love but the greatest of these is love. (1 Cor. 13:1-8; 13)

If the words of St. Paul begin to penetrate your life, you will discover the freedom love brings. The ancient Chinese used to say: "Those whom the gods would protect, they first arm with love." You will discover the truth of these words when you begin to practice Christ's command to spread the good news and to love one another. You will find that you can tolerate people again, that you can endure one more misfortune, that you can say the right word to ease another's sorrow. You will want to rise in the morning because there will be interesting, bright services to be done for others. Small services, great crusades...they are all the same when they are done for love.

If you are afraid to live because you no longer understand the world, or if you fear the pressures that come upon you and the terrifying lack of time, the words of St. Paul can help you. Read them over and over again, and then raise your heart and understand the wondrous role that can be yours in Christian Renewal.

Renewal In Christ

The man or woman who seeks renewal in Christ does not seek only his own fulfillment as an individual but seeks the salvation of the world as well. Such a human being recognizes the dangers of our society, and the headlong rush of untrained, uninspired souls into pits of loneliness and sin.

Many people today are not prone either to evil or to goodness. They do not murder their neighbors or run into stores to steal, or commit terrible sins of the flesh. Neither do they accomplish great deeds of charity or love, but some stand by and watch the murder or injury of another human being without even wanting to become involved. So many people dwell in the half-world of apathy and anxiety; longing for peace and joy of actual commitment to Christ and yet paralyzed by the lack of will to make the first step toward Him. How many of us stagger through our days without accomplishing anything, and we only barely escape from sin—perhaps because we are not tempted enough or even courageous enough to be involved in anything, good or evil. Our energies are drained by our fretting, and we have nothing to offer those who seek our aid or our example.

Walk in The Newness of Life

We no longer remember what Paul cried out with joy: "Just as Christ rose from the dead, we may also walk in the newness of life." Still we long for that newness of life, and we envy those who seem committed and energetic and alive with zeal for others.

Christ Is Love

We should take courage and have hope because Christ is eternal. He is beyond the time that limits and scars us. Christ is the God-man. He is beyond the pressures that torment us and make us fear tomorrow. Christ is love. He is never beyond our reach and never beyond the confines of our life, crowded as it may be with cares and worries. It is Christ's renewing love which can change us and supply for our limitations.

Our Limitations And Our Needs

Many times we feel these limitations deeply—the limitations that we know and feel in not understanding world problems, or neighborhood crises, or perhaps our own affairs. We live in an age of speed and we are condemned to instant decisions and sudden demands that we cannot meet unless our Christian faith is so rooted in us that we can react and commit ourselves without hesitation. We also live in an age of paradox, a time in which we can send men to the moon but cannot stop crime in the streets; an era in which we can destroy ourselves in two hours and yet cannot discover how to make trains run on time.

The more demands made on us, by civic responsibilities, parish organizations, school groups, or by our own families, the more we realize that we have terrible limitations. No matter how many labor- and time-saving devices we buy, we seem to have less and less time to be humans or Christians—unless the entire pattern of our lives is based on Christ's renewing love.

Our lack of time or ability can only lead us closer to Christ if we have the sense and courage to admit our needs. What can really happen to a human being when he openly admits that he is constantly exposed to Divine Love? What happens to a person who admits that he has little to offer, but that he can learn to rely upon God's providence? We all have need of God because we did not create ourselves and we cannot sustain ourselves. We need God for our actual existence. We are nothing. We depend upon God for all things.

Depending Upon God

This dependency upon God seems to alarm many people today because it implies that a man cannot be a law unto himself. Man is never his own end and never his own beginning—he is not even his own instrument of life. The humble person, the person who has begun to recognize his own limitations and the inadequacies of others, can take hope from the fact that he is dependent upon God. St. Paul glorified the fact of his weakness:

> As to the extraordinary revelation, in order that I might not become conceited I was given a thorn in the flesh, an angel of Satan to beat me and to keep me from getting proud. Three times I begged the Lord that this might leave me. He said to me, 'My grace is enough for you, for in weakness power reaches perfection. And so I willingly boast of my weaknesses instead, that the power of Christ may rest upon me. Therefore I am content with weakness, with mistreatment, with distress, with persecutions and difficulties for the sake of Christ; for when I am powerless, it is then that I am strong. (2 Cor. 12: 7-10)

A Metanoia—Change Of Will & Spirit

In spite of our weakness and limitations, we are the chosen ones for whom Christ came into this world. This demands, in return, a generosity and maturity of faith that will enable us to meet our responsibilities of caring for others and of changing our lives so that they reflect the Messiah's own life. It demands what Christ asked of all of us in the Sermon on the Mount: a *metanoia*, a changing of the will and the spirit that we may put aside the old ways of doing things and seek God alone. We must turn inward, recognizing that we can only change the world by changing ourselves first. For the Christian this means an act of surrender to Christ. It is learning through Mary's example to be the simple servant of the Lord who says "Fiat!"; who declares: "Do with me whatever You will for Your own glory, for the service and the salvation of others, and for the praise of Your Name."

Fulfill Our Unique Destiny

We cannot all preach to the world, or go to the missions, or even become leaders in our own parish, but we can fulfill the unique destiny which God has given us. Cardinal Newman understood this destiny when he wrote this Meditation:

God has created me to do Him some definite service; He has committed some work to me which He has not committed to another. I have my mission—I may never know it in this life, but I shall be told it in the next.

I am a link in a chain, a bond of connection between persons. He has not created me for nothing. I shall do good. I shall do His work. I shall be an angel of peace, a preacher of truth in my own place, while not intending it—If I but keep His Commandments.

Therefore, I will trust Him. Whatever, wherever I am, I can never be thrown away. If I am in sickness, my sickness may serve Him. If I am in sorrow, my sorrow may serve Him. He does nothing in vain. He knows what He is about. He may take away my friends. He may throw me among strangers. He may make me feel desolate, make my spirits sink, hide my future from me—still He knows what He is about.

We are not just mortals with weaknesses and sins and despair. We are also His beloved children, the sheep for whom He gave His life. We can dare to look heavenward because He sought us first. We can pray because He first called our names. We can call ourselves Christians because He clothed Himself in our flesh to give us that blessed title.

We Christians suffer the same misfortunes and trials of other men, but we differ from them in a special and unique manner. We have heard the Good News, the Gospel. Our ears and hearts have been opened. There are days when we do not hear any song of joy or words of love. There are times when there is darkness all about us. Still, we have heard the Gospel, and we realize that there is no end for us, no destruction that Christ cannot alter, no threat that cannot be set aside by love.

Open—Endedness in Human Life

There is always an unfinished quality to our lives, to our dreams, even to our suffering. There is an open-endedness to the human being that teases and mocks us until we realize the generous gift it is for us, whether we are a secretary in an office, a coal miner in darkness, a housewife in the kitchen, or an executive with hundreds at his command. For each one there will always be a distant horizon, a sound that reminds us that nothing has been lost, a sight of flowers or a sunset that reassures us and tells us that there is more than the petty details that have hurt us.

We all understand the open-endedness in our lives, and this sometimes annoys us and makes us ashamed, because we also realize that we waste precious moments and throw away genuine graces and gifts that He would have us spend on others. We are confused by the everyday problems we have, by the common things we see and hear, by the mundane way of doing things.

We go to Mass, and perhaps we no longer understand that service because it has changed too much for us. Perhaps we are still young and cannot see the Mass as a part of the modern scene. We come away empty, lonely, and frustrated, because deep inside we also know that we are longing for a touch of God's love, for the mystery that will overwhelm our fears and our staleness. We want to see ourselves touched by the fire that the Apostles' words describe. We only see the everyday, the fact that our families have problems, that there are bills and rising costs, that we have neighbors who do not care about anyone but themselves.

We feel pressured and threatened by forces which we cannot understand. We see our young people riot in the streets and the old abandon their dreams because they are afraid. Wars have become commonplace in many areas of the world, and suffering is the daily lot of millions. What we have taken for granted is no longer true with regard to scientific fact or security for ourselves or our families. We have learned to doubt and to fear tomorrow's destruction and waste.

We hear campaigns about ecology, about saving the earth from natural disaster, and yet we all know, deep in our hearts, that moral ecology is the actual issue. Souls are being destroyed today and people are losing their innermost integrity and dignity. This should be the major concern of us all. The ideas of love, brotherhood and peace are lost, and we stand confused and bewildered.

A True Christian

And then a single human being, a true Christian, comes into

our lives to whisper of things we have always dreamed in our hearts. A human being talks with us or works with us or just stands close by, and we recognize some deep interior beauty and joy that fills us with shame and hope in the same instant. We are ashamed because we have wasted our lives in comparison. We hope because we know that if one human being can respond to God's love in that manner, it is possible for us all to respond that blessed way.

We see the beauty of holiness and virtue, the tireless grace of devotion and the greatness of a human being who is already beyond our understanding of life because Christ's love has changed the heart and the mind of that human being into a consuming fire that can enkindle all of us. We stand in silent awe as that human being works in our lives, chiding us to actions we do not really understand or making us endure when we thought we were finished. Compelled by the intense, fierce joy that radiates to us all, we can only follow and beg a moment's glance or a gentle word that will teach us how to catch fire too.

Then, if that person moves out of our lives to some other area or into some other work, we realize that we shall never be the same again for having known him. We remember the holiness, the joy, the laughter restored, and at last, we remember the truth that is love. We try to learn more about Christ, who is the Truth, the Way, and the Life.

A Complete Renewal, Reformation, and Transformation is Necessary

In these days, when people are urged to look upon Christ as their brother, it is also wise to remember that He is Divine. Sometimes we are so stunned by the perfection of His humanity that we forget His Divinity. The act of the Incarnation can become an even greater mystery for us when we realize that Christ loved us enough to become like us, with all our miserable failings, all our weaknesses, all our trials.

> By becoming man, the Son of God became our brother, like unto us in every respect except that of sin. (Heb. 4:15)

What does Christ ask of us in return? He demands a complete conversion, complete reformation, a complete renewal of ourselves at every age. And He speaks with urgency about this renewal. Again and again Christ echoes the note of the prophets, who cried: "The Kingdom of God is at hand. Repent!" By the words repent Christ does not mean a temporary feeling of guilt or remorse. He demands a total changing of our lives, a *metanoia*, a total transformation, a true renewal of our interior spiritual life.

Christ assures us that this renewal is possible for us. Christ constitutes the New Law for us all in the Sermon of the Mount. His Beatitudes parallel the Decalogue or Ten Commandments, and yet they are entirely different from these Commandments. None of the Beatitudes deal with externals or life styles or even rituals. Christ demands something far greater from those of us who would follow Him. He demands a new interior motive of love!

> Thou shalt love the Lord Thy God, with all thy heart, and with all thy soul, and with all thy mind, and with all thy strength; this is the first commandment and the second is like unto it. Thou shalt love thy neighbor as thyself.

Love The Fulfillment of Law, and Obedience to Authority

Taken from Deuteronomy and Leviticus, the Great Commandment of Christ renews the old commandments and yet reverses the importance of everything for mankind. Christ demands pure and holy motives of love toward God and man before all else. Moral codes and ceremonies and regulations only carry out this love. Authority is the vital foundation for all acts, but love must teach us to obey authority and to make ourselves of service. Christ fulfilled the old laws faithfully, but He asked that these laws be more than vain and empty vessels. Only love can fill a man's heart and bring him to the perfection that Christ says is possible for us all.

Renewal Might be Difficult

Christ understood that such a renewal might be difficult, for the changes He would have us make strike at the root of our very natures. The old in us dies hard. Also, in these troubled times, people have abused the word love until it no longer has great significance. Love is not the physical play of two people. Love is not a song that makes the heart feel warm and glad. Love is not a parade in the streets. Read St. Paul's definition of charity again and again until you realize the strength behind the words, the sacrifice, the humility, the power of renewal for the individual. Christ understood us, and He promised that we could become saints in Him and in His Father. "With men this is impossible, but with God all things are possible" (Mt. 19:23-26).

Beatitudes Give Meaning To Life

The Sermon on the Mount, with its Beatitudes, is the greatest proof of man's right to exist on the face of the earth or in eternity. Never before has anyone given man the simple statement of his ability to raise himself above the level of the beast. This is the new song of the new man, written in hearts and not on dead stone or on cold tablets of the law. This is the divine paradox, denying mankind's common opinions and standards and elevating all that the world considers lowly or insignificant.

The Beatitudes call "ordinary life,"—the life we all fear and yet drag ourselves through year after year—"death and corruption." Christ understands the apathy we face within ourselves, the dread of others and the forgetfullness of faith and the coldness of heart that paralyze us when we know that we must strive forward for His own work. He calls all of these things "death and corruption," because He understands that they will sap our will, our strength, our joy. Christ knows it is to look upon the wretched people of the world and to see them vainly seeking for peace in their lives. They searched every road and sought out all the prophets, and yet they refused to be violent enough in their own self-discipline to discover the truth.

Christ Is Truth

Christ is truth eternal. His public life was to proclaim the

Kingdom of God and to announce that it was visible and present in Himself. The reign of God in the heart and will of a man is the Kingdom of God. It is not some distant land or some stage of development in the evolution of society. This Kingdom is possible now. A man can become a member of this Kingdom by surrendering himself completely to God in faith, by renewing his way of life, the motives that move him to action, until they reflect Christ's own way of life.

Let us remember that faith is the first necessity, it is the root of all the rest (Pope Paul VI, "Union with Christ").

And the Holy Father continues:

Your faith grows exceedingly and your charity for one another increases (Paul, II Thess. 1:13). The Church's life is as St. Paul said. It is always finding new forms grow up and draw on the fruitful sap of its divine principles, and after faith, the principle is charity.

Charity assumes the name of communion, in its general application and its modern contingencies. We shall do well to think about this word communion. It means more than community, which is something social and exterior. It means more than congregation, more than assembly, more than society, more than family, more than any kind of social union or human collectivity. It means Church.

And Church means humanity inspired and living by a single interior principle. This is not merely a matter of feeling or ideals or culture. In other words, humanity animated by a life giving Spirit, Christ's Spirit, His Grace, His Charity. These things have a twofold effect. They distinguish anyone who lives by that sanctifying principle and so give him an original way of thinking and acting, which we call the Christian way.

THE CHRISTIAN WAY

I. *The Blessed Virgin Mary, the Mother of Jesus Christ, the God-man; the Mother of Men; and the Mother of the Church.*

It has pleased God, in the fullness of time, to send His Beloved Son into the world, born of a woman so that we could become the adopted sons of God. He came down from heaven and was incarnate by the power of the Holy Spirit from the Virgin Mary.

> ... She is already prophetically foreshadowed in that victory over the serpent which was promised to our first parents after their fall into sin (cf. Gen. 3:15). Likewise she is the Virgin who is to conceive and bear a son, whose name will be called Emmanuel (cf. Is. 7:14; Mic. 5:2-3; Mt. 1:22-23). (Vatican II, *The Church*, Art. 55)

It was the wish of the Father that the consent of Mary should precede the Incarnation, and for this purpose was the Archangel Gabriel sent to her. He greeted her with the words, "Hail, full of grace, the Lord is with you. Blessed are you among women." (Lk. 1:28)

The Immaculate Conception

She was to give to the world that very life which renews all things; therefore she was enriched by God with gifts befitting that role. The words, "Hail, full of grace," means that she received the gift of Immaculate Conception.

> It is no wonder, then, that the usage prevailed among the holy Fathers whereby they called the mother of God entirely holy and free from all stain of sin, fashioned by the Holy Spirit into a kind of new substance and new creature. Adorned from the first instant of her conception with the splendors of an entirely unique holiness, the Virgin of Nazareth is, on God's command, greeted by an angel messenger as "Full of Grace." (Vat. II, *The Church*, 56)

Be It Done Unto Me According to Your Word

When Mary heard the greeting she was disturbed and troubled. The angel told her not to be fearful, that God has chosen her to bring forth a son, who would be called Jesus. She asked him how this could be since she did not know man. He told her that the Holy Spirit would overshadow her and that the holy one born of her would be called the Son of God. He told her that Elizabeth, her cousin, was also with child, because nothing is impossible to God. Then Mary replied: "Behold the handmaid of the Lord, be it done to me according to your word" (Lk 1:29-38). Thus Mary became the Mother of God and Mother of the Redeemer.

> At the message of the angel, the Virgin Mary received the Word of God in her heart and in her body, and gave Life to the world. Hence she is acknowledged and honored as being truly the Mother of God and Mother of the Redeemer. Redeemed in an especially sublime manner by reason of the merits of her Son, and united to Him by a close and indissoluble tie, she is endowed with the supreme office and dignity of being the Mother of the Son of God. As a result she is also the favorite daughter of the Father and the temple of the Holy Spirit. Because of this gift of sublime grace she far surpasses all other creatures, both in heaven and on earth. (Vat. II, *The Church*, 53)

Union Between Mary and Jesus

The union between Mary and Jesus was evident from the moment of Christ's virginal conception until His death on the cross. This union was so close that Mary devoted herself entirely as the handmaid of the Lord to the person and work of Jesus. Along with Jesus and in subordination to Him she served the mystery of redemption.

> Rightly therefore the holy Fathers see her used by God not merely in a passive way, but as cooperating in the work of human salvation, through free faith and obedience. (Vat. II, *The Church*, 56)

Soon after the Incarnation, Mary went in haste to her kinswoman Elizabeth. The Holy Spirit inspired Elizabeth to greet

Mary with the words, "Blessed are you among women and blessed is the fruit of your womb! And how have I deserved that the mother of my Lord should come to me? For behold, the moment that the sound of your greeting came to my ears, the babe in my womb leapt for joy. And blessed is she who has believed, because the things promised her by the Lord shall be accomplished" (Lk 1: 42-45).

Sharing of Mary In Redemptive Plan of Christ

This was the first manifestation of Mary working in the plan of salvation. Throughout Christ's life on earth she continued to associate herself with Christ's redemptive plan. At the birth of Christ she gladly showed her Son to the shepherds and magi. When she presented Jesus in the temple, Simeon foretold that a sword of sorrow would pierce her soul, and that Christ would be a sign of contradiction so that thoughts might be revealed from the hearts of many. At finding Jesus in the temple she did not understand what was meant by His remark that "He must be about His Father's business." She kept all these things in her heart to ponder over them. In Christ's public life she made significant appearances. At Cana, while at the wedding feast, she was moved with pity, and through her intercession Jesus worked His first miracle. And when He was preaching she received His praise when He declared all blessed who hear and keep His word. This she always faithfully did. (cf. Vat. II, *The Church*, 57-58)

Mary stood beneath the cross, suffering grievously with her Son, uniting herself with Him and giving loving consent to the immolation. It was there that Christ gave her to us to be our mother.

> The Blessed Virgin advanced in her pilgrimage of faith, and loyally persevered in her union with her Son unto the cross. There she stood, in keeping with the Divine plan (cf. Jn. 19:25), suffering grievously with her only-begotten Son. There she united herself with a maternal heart to His sacrifice, and lovingly consented to the immolation of this victim which she herself had brought forth. Finally the same Christ Jesus dying on the cross gave her as a mother to His disciple. This He did when He said: "Woman, behold your son" (Jn. 19: 26-27). (Vat. II, *The Church*, 58)

After Christ's death, resurrection, and ascension into heaven, we see Mary continue her role. She was with the Apostles in the upper room, imploring God to send forth the Holy Spirit promised by her Son Jesus.

> We see the Apostles before the day of Pentecost 'Continuing with one mind in prayer with the women and Mary, the Mother of Jesus, and with His brethren' (Acts 1:14). We see Mary prayerfully imploring the gift of the Spirit, who had already overshadowed her in the Annunciation. (Vat. II, *The Church*, 59)

Mary's Role From Heaven

Finally we see the Immaculate Virgin taken up to heaven, body and soul. There she was glorified by the Lord as Queen of all. Her role in the history of salvation did not end with the completion of her life on earth, but was to continue in heaven because she is our mother in the order of grace.

> In an utterly singular way she cooperated by her obedience, faith, hope, and burning charity in the Savior's work of restoring supernatural life to souls. For this reason she is a *Mother to us in the order of grace*. (Vat. II, *The Church*, 61) For, taken up to heaven, she did not lay aside this saving role, but by her manifold acts of intercession continues to win for us the gifts of eternal salvation. (Vat. II, *The Church*, 62)

Role of Mary To Foster Union of Faithful With Christ

Mary's maternal duty toward us is not intended to diminish the mediation of Christ in any way. Rather, it is to show its power because all the saving actions of the Blessed Mother flow forth from the superabundance of Christ's merits. They do not impede the immediate union of the faithful with Christ. Rather, they are to foster this union. Thus Mary can rightly be invoked under the titles of Advocate and Mediatrix. Yet, these are to be understood as taking nothing away from the role of Christ as Mediator because there is only one Mediator between God and man—Christ Jesus. Yet, the subordinate role of Mary is recognized and fostered by the Church.

The Church does not hesitate to profess this subordinate role of Mary. She experiences it continuously and commends it to the faithful, so that encouraged by this maternal help they may more closely adhere to the Mediator and Redeemer. (Vat. II, *The Church*, 62)

We should turn to Mary without fear because she is our model, as well as the model of the Church. She brings us to Christ.

Proper Devotion to Mary

The Church has always honored Mary and devotion to her has spread throughout the Catholic world. It is the wish of Vatican Council II that devotion to Mary continue and be fostered so that we may come to know, love, and glorify her son Jesus, and that His commands be faithfully observed. The Council has warned that we should avoid the falsity of exaggeration in our devotion, but also the excess of narrow-mindedness. Our devotion to Mary should proceed from a true faith, a healthy and upright attitude, so that we may further the glory of God. We should uphold and foster devotions that have been practiced and treasured by the teaching authority of the Church down through the centuries.

Mary—Our Mother

Mary is Our Mother, and the children that deny their mother are orphaned and lost in the wilderness of their own misery. No one attempting to enter into the spiritual life or into spiritual development can afford to ignore this Model of Virtue, this Pillar of Honor, this Rose of Purity. None of the saints was stupid enough to ignore the Mother of God. We must turn ourselves back again to the Vision of Her Loveliness and take hope, and we must restore her lustre in the eyes of our children for the hope of the years ahead.

Let us heed the words of Vatican Council II and pray to Mary; let us put on the mind of Mary; let us do everything in, through, and with Mary. Let us consecrate ourselves to her Maternal, Immaculate and Sorrowful Heart. Let us do this that we may be filled with her love, that we may imitate her virtues, and that she may bring us to Christ.

II. *Jesus Christ, the Son of God, the God-Man, the Redeemer*

> In the beginning was the Word, and the Word was with God; and the Word was God. He was in the beginning with God. All things were made through Him, and without Him was made nothing that was made. In Him was life and the life was the light of men. And the light shines in the darkness; and the darkness grasped it not. There was a man, one sent from God, whose name was John. This man came as a witness, to bear witness concerning the light, that all might believe through him. He was not himself the light, but was to bear witness to the light. It was the true light that enlightens every man who comes into the world. He was in the world and the world was made through Him, and the world knew Him not. He came into His own, and His own received Him not. But to as many as received Him He gave the power of becoming sons of God; to those who believe in His Name: Who were born not of blood, nor of the will of the flesh, nor of the will of man, but of God.
>
> And the Word was made flesh, and dwelt among us. And we saw His glory—glory as of the only-begotten of the Father—full of grace and of truth. John bore witness concerning Him, and cried, "This was He of whom I said, 'He who is to come after me has been set above me.'" And of His fullness we have all received, grace for grace. For the Law was given through Moses; grace and truth come through Jesus Christ. No one has at any time seen God. The only-begotten Son, Who is in the bosom of the Father, He has revealed Him. (Jn. 1: 1-18)

In the fullness of time, God the Father sent His only-begotten Son into the world. He took flesh of the ever Virgin Mary and dwelt among us, through the power of the Holy Spirit, and His name was called, Jesus.

> God in turn exalted Him above all else, and bestowed upon Him that Name which is above every other name, whose dignity requires that at the mention of Jesus' Name every knee must bend throughout the heavens and on earth and under the earth, and every tongue proclaim the glory of God the Father: 'Jesus Christ is Lord!' (Phil. 2: 9-11)

God now speaks to us through His Son (Heb. 1: 1-2; Jn. 1: 18), and He speaks of Himself. Through Christ, He tells us that there is one God in three Divine Persons, the Father, the Son, and the Holy Spirit. "The Catholic faith is this, that we worship one God in Trinity and Trinity in Unity." (St. Athanasius)

> The life of God expresses itself in the activity of the Divine Intellect and of the Divine Will. The Father in knowing Himself, declares and expresses that knowledge in the Infinite Word; this act is simple and eternal; and the Son, begotten of the Father, is like and equal to Him, because the Father communicates to the Son His Nature, life and perfections, and thus, the Father and the Son are drawn to each other by a common and mutual love. Each gives Himself to the other, and this mutual love which springs from the Father and the Son, as from one source, is in God a subsisting love, a Person distinct from the other two Persons; He is the Holy Spirit ... Like the Father and the Son, He is God; He possesses like Them and with Them, one and the same Divine Nature, equal knowledge, equal power, equal majesty, equal goodness. (Abbot Marmion)

Christ came into the world to reveal the love of the Father to all men.

> By an utterly free and mysterious decree of His own wisdom and goodness, the eternal Father, created the whole world. His plan was to dignify men with a participation in His own Divine life. God the Father did not abandon men after they had fallen in Adam, but ceaselessly offered them help to salvation, in anticipation of Christ the Redeemer, "Who is the image of the invisible God, the first-born of every creature" (Col. 1:15). All the elect, before time began, the Father foreknew and predestined to become conformed to the image of His Son, that He should be the first-born among many brethren." (Rom. 8:29) (Vatican II, *The Church*, 2)

God's Plan For Man's Salvation

In Jesus Christ, His Son, God the Father revealed the beauty and the completeness of His love for man. The mystery of God's plan for man's salvation was totally revealed in the person of Jesus. To understand the plan, then, we must understand Jesus. Christ was the God-Man. He who was God became, in a single moment of history, a man as well.

We have only to read Holy Scripture to see that Christ was a man as well as God. Looking at Christ as a person, one gets the impression that He was only man. He lived as a man, feasted with the common people at wedding celebrations, and suffered fatigue. The Apostles did not recognize His Divinity until Peter proclaimed Him to be the Messiah, the Son of the living God. His own towns people in Nazareth said, "Is this not the carpenter's son?" Christ claimed to be God and that is why He was put to death. He also proved He was God by His sinless life; His miracles, which He worked through His own power; by forgiving sins—His enemies said, "Who is this that He forgives sins?"

The Mystery of The Incarnation

We believe that in Christ there are two natures—human and Divine, but there is only one Person—a Divine Person. This is called the Mystery of the Incarnation. He became man so that He could redeem us from our sins. If He had been only God, the Second Person of the Blessed Trinity, He could never have redeemed us, He could not have been our Mediator, He could not have suffered or died on the cross. At the Incarnation, the Second Person of the Blessed Trinity assumed a human nature from the Blessed Virgin Mary through the power of the Holy Spirit. Thus He could redeem us. He could be our Mediator. He could suffer in His human nature, and He could die on the cross. We attribute an action to the person, therefore we can say that God suffered for us, that God died for us, that God saved us.

Who is Christ? Peoples' Opinions

Again, who is Christ? Christ Himself asked His disciples this fateful question: "Who do people say the Son of Man is?" (Mt. 16-13). Christ speaks of Himself not in the first person, but in the third person, when He calls Himself the Son of Man. Matthew used this expression many times in his Gospel, not only to show His lowliness, but also His greatness. He is Lord of the Sabbath (Mt. 10:23). He has power to forgive sins (Mt. 9:6). By calling Himself the Son of Man, Jesus allows the mystery of Christ to shine through, that is, He is the Son of God.

The answers given by the people were sorely mistaken because they showed that they did not understand the true identity of

Christ. All the disciples agreed that people considered Him to be John the Baptist, others Elias, Jeremiah, or one of the prophets. (Mt. 16:14)

Peter's Confession—Revelation of Heavenly Father

When Christ asked the important question, "But who do you say I am?" (Mt. 16:15), only Simon Peter answered: "You are the Messiah, the Son of the living God." (Mt. 16:17) Christ's reply makes it clear that Peter's confession of Christ's Messiahship was equivalent to a confession of His Divine Sonship, because it was possible only through a special revelation of the Father. "Blessed are you, Simon Bar-Jona, for flesh and blood has not revealed this to you but My Father Who is in Heaven." (Mt. 16:17)

Purpose of Jesus Christ's Life

After we know who Christ was, the next logical question is, what was the purpose of Jesus' life? The first and most evident reason for Christ's life is to proclaim the Gospel. He came to proclaim the truth. His life is God's Word to mankind. Is that all? No! We may not forget the tragic end of His earthly life, His death on the cross. Nor may we overlook the fact that He knew how He would die, when He would die, how much suffering He would have to bear. The Gospel narrative is full of the prophetic foreknowledge of Jesus about the fate that awaited Him (cf. Lk. 8: 31; 9: 31; 10: 33ff.) Christ knew when His hour would come (Cf. Jn. 2:4; 7:30; 13:1; 17:1) And the prophecies of the past and future were ever before His Divine eye (cfr. Matthew's Gospel; Jn. 13:18; 15:25; Lk. 24:25)

The Suffering Servant

Jesus was willing to undergo suffering and death on the cross for our salvation. We see this in many Gospel testimonies. When He tells his disciples that He must go to Jerusalem, to suffer greatly and be killed there, Peter protests and tries to persuade

Jesus not to accept this fate, but Jesus reproves him severely. (Mt. 16:21-23) When Peter wishes to defend Christ in the Garden of Gethsemane, He again reproves Peter: "Put your sword into its sheath; shall I not drink the cup which the Father has given Me?" (Jn 18:11; Heb. 9:14) St.. Mark also tells us: "For the Son of Man came not to be served, but to serve, and to give His life as a ransom for many." (Mk. 10:45; Is. 53:10ff)

The vocation of Christ was to carry the burdens of mankind within His heart. We can readily imagine the inner sufferings of Jesus, which He bore all His life as a foretaste of His Passion. His inner feelings and sufferings were expressed openly in the scene at Gethsemane. (Lk. 22:43)

Christ's Sinless Life

The moral character of Christ was beyond reproach, and the tender nature of His Heart was revealed throughout His life. Jesus was kind with a Divine kindness (Cf. Mk. 10: 17-19-21). He had compassion and understanding of other people's pain and distress (Mt. 11:28). He was able to comprehend, forgive, and rehabilitate. St. Paul understood and magnificently defined Jesus Christ as "the man for others." By saying this he shows that he had a deep insight into the secret of Christ's earthly life, the purpose of the Incarnation, and he tells us to what extent Jesus was for others: "Jesus died for our sins in accordance with the scriptures" (1 Cor. 15:3).

Jesus, Our Savior

Jesus, Whose name means Savior, came into the world to save us. He saved us by becoming a victim for our redemption. This mystery of abasement merges with the mystery of His sublimation which is the Incarnation. It enters into the eternal plan, fully revealed only with Christ, or God's love for us. (Col. 1:26) Without this revelation we could not know anything about ourselves. It enters into the sacrificial value of Our Lord's passion, which is universal and replaces the expiration which was impossible for us to do. (Cf. Pope Paul, "Jesus Came to Suffer")

The final and total work of Christ is the Redemption. It enters human destiny to establish a free and highly auspicious relationship of each of us personally with our Lord Jesus Christ.

> Christ loved us and gave Himself up for me, St. Paul proclaimed (Eph. 5:2; Gal. 2:20). For me—here, beloved Brothers and Sons, Christian life begins for each of us, a life of love, which comes to us: light, fire, blood of Christ, in the Spirit: and love, which goes from us, as it can with all its strength, towards Christ and in search of brothers, still in the Spirit. Amen. (Pope Paul, "Jesus Came to Suffer")

That We May Be One

Christ wished that we remain united with Him. At the Last Supper He was thinking of the mystery of grace, that is, of charity, which is "a certain friendship between man and God" (St. Thomas, 11-11ae, 23:5). He prayed to His Father that we may be one, that we may be united into our family—the Family of God.

> Holy Father, keep them in Thy Name, whom Thou hast given me that they may be one, as We are one... And not for them only do I pray, but for those also who through their word shall believe in Me; that they may all be one, as Thou Father in Me, and I in Thee, that they also may be one in Us, that the world may believe that Thou has sent me. And the glory which Thou hast given Me, I have given to them; that they may be one, as We also are one. I in them and Thou in Me; that they may be made perfect in one; and the world may know that Thou hast sent Me and hast loved them as Thou hast loved Me. (Jn. 11: 20-33)

Eternal Relationship

Christ promised that the supernatural relationship He had established would last forever, even after His death and resurrection.

> Our Lord's thoughts in this regard are very clear. He established a lasting link between Himself and His own, and neither His death nor His resurrection would break that link. On His side it would be permanent, and He wished it to be permanent on their side also, but also free and personal. (Pope Paul, "Union With Christ")

United in The Spirit

The object of the incarnation, passion, death and resurrection of Our Lord was to gather all the children of God together in the same spirit and in the same indwelling of the Holy Spirit.

Pope Paul explains this in his talk on "Union with Christ."

> We must be in vital communion with Christ. The personal factor is the one that matters here. It is something intimate and spiritual, something that goes on in the depths of our being. Our consciousness cannot get to those depths, except through faith and through some rare and imperfect experiences. The mystics know most about this, yet each of us ought to be able to say, 'I live, no longer I, but Christ lives on in me' (Gal. 2:20). This sense of interior communion with Christ, or of personal union with Him, of His indwelling in our souls (cf Eph. 3: 17), ought to be always alive in us, like a burning lamp.

Through Mary, we should make a personal commitment to Christ. Mary helps us to know and love her Son, Jesus. We fall in love with Jesus. We are able to do this since Christ is a person, and a person to person relationship can develop. Our life takes on a new dimension and we begin to realize the importance of our spiritual life. He brings us to know and love the Father.

> Just Father, the world has not known Thee, but I have known Thee, and these have known that Thou hast sent Me. And I have made known to them Thy Name, and will make It known, in order that the love with which Thou hast loved Me may be in them, and I in them. (Jn. 17:25-26)

If we love Christ, He and the Father will come to us:

> If anyone love Me, He will keep My word, and My Father will love him, and We will come to him and make Our abode with him. He who does not love Me does not keep My words. And the word that you have heard is not Mine, but the Father's who sent Me. (Jn. 14: 23-24)

A quasi-intellectual awareness of the indwelling of God the Father and the Son develops in one's consciousness. Christ said if we love Him the Father and He would come to us, and then He would ask the Father to send the Holy Spirit to come and dwell within us. We all know that we receive the gift of the indwelling of the Holy Trinity in our souls at baptism, but here we are speaking of something else, and that is, we actually become aware of the Presence of God within us. We can truly say that we have received the "baptism of the Spirit."

It has pleased God to send His son to us through Mary by the power of the Holy Spirit. We are to go back to Him through Mary with Christ in the Spirit. This is what we mean by total Christian Renewal.

III. *The Holy Spirit, the God of Love, Paraclete, Advocate, and Sanctifier*

Pentecost—The Fire of Love

St. Luke tells us, in the opening words of the Acts of the Apostles, that in his Gospel he had written "all the things that Jesus began to do and to teach until the day He . . . was taken up to heaven." The words and works of Christ were only a beginning. They must continue down through the centuries until the end of the world. It is He and only He who can continue them. But how? Pentecost is the answer—it is the birthday of the Church and, as it were, a second birth of Jesus Christ.

After Christ's Ascension into heaven, the Apostles, together with the disciples and Mary, gathered in an upper room, called the cenacle, to pray and to wait for the fulfillment of the Lord's promise. He had instructed them to "Wait here in the city, until you are clothed with power from on high." (Lk. 24:49)

They could not understand what the power would be, and so Christ instructed them in this also:

> If you love Me and keep My commandments, then at My request the Father will give you another Paraclete to be with you forever—the Spirit of Truth. The world cannot accept Him because it neither sees nor recognizes Him; you can recognize Him because He remains with you and He will be within you. I shall not leave you orphans: I am coming back to you. There is just a little time before the world loses sight of Me; but you can see Me because I have life and you will have life. On that day you yourself will recognize that I am in My Father, and you are in Me, and I am in you. Whoever keeps the commandments that he has from Me is the man who loves Me; and the man who

loves Me will be loved by My Father, and I shall love him and reveal Myself to him. (Jn. 14:15-22)

The birthday of the Church is the feast of Pentecost. On this day the Holy Spirit descended upon the disciples. The name Pentecost is an ancient one, originally celebrated by the Jewish people approximately fifty days after the Passover festival.

The coming of the Paraclete, the Holy Spirit, marks not only the founding of the Church but the striking realization of the most Holy Trinity as well. This understanding did not come quickly for mankind. In the early days, when the Jewish people were being trained as God's chosen people, they learned only that there was one God. There could not be three Gods but one, transcendent, all-knowing, all-powerful. This concept of one God came down through history with the Jewish people, and they were faithful to it as a nation, enduring slavery, persecution, destruction on all sides because of their steadfastness.

Then the mystery of the Trinity was revealed to mankind in the person of Jesus Christ. Christ made known the Trinity in His words and in His Life. He made man understand that He was the true Son of God, sent by the Father to save all men. He also promised the Holy Spirit to His Apostles: the Divine Spirit who proceeds from the Father and the Son. The Father desired the salvation of all men, so the Son became Man to further the Divine Plan, and the Holy Spirit still guides the Church and dwells in all of us. Thus we may call God our Father, pray to the Son, and serve in the Church. (cf. Vat. II, *The Church*, Art. 2-4)

The Church of God—Gift to Man

The Church holds the offices of teacher, priest or sanctifier, and pastor or ruler. To ensure the proper functioning of these offices, Christ gave the Church the gift of the Holy Spirit. God the Father and God the Son sent the Holy Spirit to dwell in the Church.

"On the feast of Pentecost, we celebrate a mystery which is forever renewed in the Church and in our souls: The mystery of the indwelling of God, the reign of the law of love, which suc-

ceeds the law of bondage and fear." (Rom. 8:15)
As Pope Paul explains so carefully:

> What does 'Church' mean? Church means a summons, a summons from whom? From God. To whom is this summons addressed? To mankind.
> The word at once represents a great and mysterious phenomenon. Is there a story behind the phenomenon? There is. First of all, that of the Old Testament. Then there is that of the New Testament, which is our own story, and is marked by the coming of Christ, the word of God made man, 'to gather the children of God who had been scattered.' (Jn 11:52), and by the extension of the summons to the whole of mankind. This word 'Church' condenses in a focal point, as it were, all the wealth, the originality and the truth of religion and human destinies.
> If the call comes from God, the initiative is His; the plan involved in it is His, and the love that is immediately revealed in it is His. We ought to reread St. Paul's letter to the Ephesians, especially the first and second chapters ... They will give us an idea of the Church as a call from God, of a religion which does not start from man but from God, but which does not remain one-sided, incomplete and all too often an ineffective and erroneous religion, like human attempts at religion, but constitutes the sure relationship, true dialogue, finally a communion, consequently salvation and blessedness.
> The Church is mankind which has been called and has responded. It is the assembly of people called by God in Christ. It is the Kingdom of God; it is the People of God, it is the congregation of believers. (cf. St. Jerome in Ephesians; P.L. 26, 534). (Pope Paul VI, "The Church-The Sacrament of Christ," 2-5)

As St. Peter explained:

> But you are a chosen race, a royal household, a priesthood, a holy nation, a people God takes as His own, that you may declare the praises of Him who called you out of darkness into His wonderful light. Once not a people, you are now God's people; once there was no mercy for you, but now you have found mercy. (1 Pet. 2: 9-10)

Thus we can understand that the People of God "was established by Christ as a fellowship of life, charity and truth; it is also used by Him as an instrument for the redemption of all, and is sent forth into the whole world as the light of the world and the salt of the earth." (Cf. Mt. 5:13-16) (Vat. II, *The Church*, 9).

All of us who have been invited by Christ to become members of His Church, through baptism, receive the Holy Spirit in Him and so become united one to the other. We are able to call ourselves God's children and heirs and are bound together by Christ's command of Love.

> Therefore, if you hearken to My voice and keep My covenant, you shall become My special possession, dearer to Me than all other people, though all the earth is mine. (Ex. 19:5)

And the Bishops at the Vatican Council defined the role of the Church:

> The Church strives energetically and constantly to bring all humanity with all its riches back to Christ its Head in the unity of His Spirit. (Vat. II, *The Church*, 13)
> This messianic people, although it does not actually include all men, and may more than once look like a small flock, is nonetheless a lasting and sure deed of unity, hope and salvation for the whole human race. (Vat. II, *The Church*, 9)

It would seem that many modern Catholics have forgotten the great heritage that is within the Church and have almost lost sight of the basic role the Church plays in the world. We recite a profession of faith, a creed that lists "One Lord, one faith, one baptism." There has never been any other civilization, any other group or society so closely united, because there has never been a Mystical Body of Christ before.

The Mystical Body of Christ

The Mystical Body of Christ as we now understand it came from St. Paul's concept of Christ. The word mystical is used to distinguish the Church from the actual physical person of Christ which is enthroned in heaven. Even though we Christians, who make up the Mystical Body, are in reality united to Christ's physical body, it is a mystical union that forms the Mystical Body to which we belong. By the same token, the word mystical distinguishes the Church from a purely physical body in the natural order. Our natural bodies exist only in and for one person. The Mystical Body of Christ embraces all persons and yet leaves each person distinct and unique as God created him.

Finally, we call the Mystical Body a mystical entity to distinguish it from a purely moral body. This means that we are more than just a group of people coming together for a common reason. We are united to and in Christ, in a single purpose. We are also much more. The Mystical Body embraces all of us, but it also contains an internal principle of unity, the Holy Spirit, which unites the members in a distinct manner far beyond any moral order or union.

The Mystical Body of Christ—St. Paul was the first to use this beautiful phrase. Paul was a man of the Old Testament, and yet he committed himself to the Son of God who gave us the Gospel, the good news that we now call the New Testament. He well understood that there was a difference between these two separate people, and he tried to summon an image that would explain that the People of God were no longer distinguished just by being born of so many ancient tribes. The distinction was no longer racial or ethnic.

> There is neither Jew nor Greek; there is neither slave nor freeman; there is neither male nor female. For you are all one in Christ Jesus. (Gal. 3:28)
> And the bread we break, is it not the partaking of the body of the Lord? Because the bread is one, we though many, are one body, all of us who partake of one bread. (1 Cor. 11, 10: 16-17)

When St. Paul speaks of the *body,* he does not mean just the physical nature, distinct from the soul. The phrase "Body of Christ" means the whole being to Paul, all of Christ, Christ entire. The union between the creature called man and the Redeemer, Jesus, is so real to Paul that he actually calls it a marriage, like the union between husband and wife. (cf. 1 Cor. 6: 15-17) This means that Paul understood the union between the soul and Christ to be more than some vague, dark awareness of Jesus; it was an actual union.

This genuine union of the soul with Christ led to the conclusion that the Church, the assembly of souls united with Christ, is the body of Christ. Read Paul's Epistles to the Ephesians and to the Colossians. Here, for the first time, Christ is called the head of the body, which is the Church. As the head, Christ is the only source of life to the members. As the head, Christ is the only nurturing for the souls in genuine union—the Church.

> In that body, the life of Christ is poured into the believers, who through the Sacraments, are united in a hidden and real way to Christ Who suffered and was glorified ... "For just as the body is one and has many members, and all the members of the body, though many, are one body, so it is with Christ.' (1 Cor. 12:12) Also, in the building up of Christ's body, various members and functions have their part to play—giving the body unity through himself and through his power and inner joining of the members, this same Spirit produces and urges love among the believers ... The Head of this Body is Christ ... By the greatness of His power He rules the things of heaven and the things on earth, and with all His surpassing perfection and way of acting He fills the whole body with the riches of His glory. (Cf Eph 1: 18-23) (Vat. II, *The Church*, 7)

St. Augustine understood the same thing about the Church when he wrote:

> The Church is a body of Christ and by charity is brought into unity. The temple of God is the Holy Church, namely the universal Church in heaven and on earth; all the faithful being from the beginning of the world to the end. Now the head of this body is Christ, the soul is the Holy Spirit. The entire Christ is both head and body.
> There is a common life among Christians. Their offices are different, their life is common; that the faithful are the children of the martyrs who intercede for us and whom we must reverence. We are also the fruit of their dear labor.

We are the People of God, the fruit of the blessed martyrs. But we belong to the Mystical Body of Christ. Called by Christ to be a part of His Mystical Body, brought into that Body through baptism, we are a rare and privileged people. God the Father is our Father. Jesus Christ, the God-Man, is our Redeemer and Brother. The Holy Spirit is our Sanctifier. Mary is our true spiritual mother.

The Pilgrim Church

The Council of Bishops meeting at Vatican II, with a sense of historical consciousness, has brought back to life an ancient term: *The Pilgrim Church*. The Constitution on the Sacred Liturgy defines the Church as "present in the world and still a pilgrim." St. Augustine similarly described the Church:

> The Church continues its pilgrimage among the world's persecution and God's consolations." (*City of God*, 18)

Pope Paul VI, in his talk on the Deposit of Faith, is quite explicit about the Pilgrim Church, and it is well to read his words and to discover the ancient and yet refreshingly new concepts there:

> The image of the pilgrim is clear and tells us many quite important things, yet they are not simple or easily understood. Still, it is well to keep them in mind. The image of the pilgrimage tells us that the Church has a twofold life. One is in time, that in which we now find ourselves. The other is beyond time, in eternity, that to which our pilgrimage is headed. Awareness of the fact that the Church exists in a changeability of time—as does every creature and every individual ...will make us realize, not only in a speculative way but also on the practical and moral plane, the unstable and frail nature of everything that goes to make up our present world.
> The pilgrim Church means that Church passing through time with these two characteristics which distinguish its history. One is that the Church has certain values which must be safeguarded. Those values are the faith, grace, Christ living in the mystery of His Mystical Body which is the Church itself. That is to say that the Church is alive and bears the Divine guarantee that the adversities of history shall not be able to destroy Her and this adventurous but unconquered pilgrimage shall last 'even until the end of the world.' (Mt. 28:20)
> The other characteristic is certainty that the Church's pilgrimage through the centuries has a fixed goal. That shall be the final, glorious and endless meeting with Jesus Christ living at the Father's right hand, that is to say, in the indescribable mystery of the Most Holy Trinity. This goal gives the Church the sense that it is near and almost imminent, it inspires the final invocation, 'Amen. Come, Lord Jesus.' (Pope Paul VI, "Deposit of Faith," 7)

The Mission of the Pilgrim Church

The Pilgrim Church, the People of God have a mission to fulfill. This mission is a simple command: to extend the Kingdom of God on earth. All who have been baptized have this mission to perform in their daily lives, in their acts of consecration, in their holiness. The power to execute this mission is given through the Sacraments and the sacred ministries of the Church. The Holy Spirit leads and purifies the People of God. By these gifts they are made fit and ready to undertake the various tasks and offices which contribute to the building and to the renewal of the Church. (cf. Vat. II, *The Church*, 11).

> The Church strives energetically and constantly to bring all humanity with all its riches back to Christ its Head in the unity of the Spirit. (Vat. II *The Church*, 13)

The Pilgrim Church—Hierarchy And The Faithful

The Pilgrim Church has a two fold dimension: the hierarchy and the faithful. Both must work in harmony for the building of the Kingdom of God on earth. The hierarchy is to lead, instruct, govern, and sanctify. Above all it is to be of service to the People of God, to aid them in the work of their salvation. The faithful are to respect, love, and obey the hierarchy, and also to help it fulfill its mission.

We see clearly in Scriptural writings that Christ intended to establish a hierarchically structured Church. We also see that the Apostles understood this and carried out the intentions of Christ by appointing successors as bishops of the Church. In Scripture we also see that priests, deacons, and lay people helped the bishops to fulfill their mission given to them by Christ. This has been the Church down through the centuries, and it is the same today. Thus we can say that the Church is hierarchically structured—yesterday, today, and in the future until the end of time because it was the Will of Christ that it be so.

It is important to understand the hierarchically structured Church founded by Christ so that we may understand the role of the Holy Father, the bishops, priests and deacons who make up the hierarchy.

After Peter proclaimed that Christ was the Son of the living God, Christ answered, "... and I say to you: you are Peter (Rock), and on this rock I will build My Church; and the gates of the underworld will not prevail against it." (Mt. 16:18)

The Rock—The Papacy

This reply of Christ referred to Peter's primacy, and not to Peter's character. Peter was not as firm as a rock; he was a simple fisherman, a kind and well-intentioned person, but also rash and impulsive and at times even cowardly. He was not "the disciple whom Jesus loved;" that was John. Any one of the Apostles could have been equally suited for the office intended for Peter. The Lord had a singular purpose in singling out Peter. It was a Divine dispensation which disregarded human faculties. It was a sovereign gift of grace. Peter was to receive the charism of being the "Rock" of the Church.

In the Bible the word "rock" signifies firmness. Christ uses this image only twice and both times in reference to Peter. The first time, when Andrew brought his brother to meet Jesus, Christ said, "You are Simon, Son of John; you will be called Kephas"— which means "Rock." (Jn. 1:42) The second time was at Caesarea Philippi when Peter said Christ was the Messiah. Christ then changed Peter's name. It is a special feature of Scripture that a name bestowed by God is tied to an office, a task, a function which had been performed or will be performed by the recipient in the future. For example, in the Old Testament, Jacob received the name "Israel" which means "Wrestler of God"—"Henceforth your name shall be not Jacob but Israel; for you have wrestled with God and men, and you have been victorious." (Gen. 32:28) Or, in the case of Abram, who according to God's promise would become the father of many nations. "Henceforth your name shall not be Abram—but Abraham, for I shall make you the father of many nations." (Gen. 17:5)

The Pope—Infallible Teacher

What office, task, or function did Jesus give to Peter when He called him "Rock"? From the tone of Sacred Scripture, we can see that in Christ's mind it referred to the infallible teaching of Peter. By promising to build His Church on the "Rock," Christ meant to say that Peter would hold the office of infallible teacher in the Church as long as the Church exists. The image of "Rock" used by Christ extends beyond the life of Simon Peter. It implies succession in this office of infallible teacher. Simon Peter will have successors in this office until the end of the world because Christ promised His Church would last until the end of time.

> In order that the episcopate itself might be one and undivided, He placed Blessed Peter over the other apostles, and instituted in him a permanent and visible source and foundation of unity of faith and fellowship. And all this teaching about the institution, the perpetuity, the force and reason for the sacred primacy of the Roman Pontiff and of his infallible teaching authority, this sacred Synod again proposes to be firmly believed by all the faithful. (Vat. II, *The Church*, 18)

The Roman Pontiff exercises this power of infallibility whenever he makes a definitive pronouncement about faith and morals, which are contained in the deposit of Divine Revelation.

> This infallibility with which the Divine Redeemer willed His Church to be endowed in defining a doctrine of faith and morals extends as far as extends the deposit of divine revelation, which must be religiously guarded and faithfully expounded. This is the infallibility which the Roman Pontiff, the head of the college of bishops, enjoys in virtue of his office, when, as the supreme shepherd and teacher of all the faithful, who confirms his brethren in their faith (cf. Lk. 22:32), he proclaims by a definitive act some doctrine of faith and morals. Therefore his definitions, of themselves, and not from the consent of the Church, are justly styled irreformable, for they are pronounced with the assistance of the Holy Spirit, an assistance promised to him in blessed Peter. Therefore, they need no approval of others, nor do they allow an appeal to any other judgment. For then the Roman Pontiff is not pronouncing judgment as a private person. Rather, as the supreme teacher of the universal Church, as one in whom the charism of the infallibility of the Church herself is individually present, he is expounding on a doctrine of Catholic Faith. (Vat. II, *The Church*, 25)

Pope—Pastor of the Universal Church

The Roman Pontiff as Pastor of the whole Church has universal power which he can exercise freely.

> For in virtue of his office, that is, as Vicar of Christ and pastor of the whole Church, the Roman Pontiff has full, supreme, and universal power over the Church, and he can always exercise this power freely. (Vat. II, *The Church* 22)

When the Roman Pontiff speaks on matters of faith and morals, religious submission must be given, even if he is not speaking *ex cathedra*.

> In matters of faith and morals... religious submission of will and of mind must be shown in a special way to the authentic teaching authority of the Roman Pontiff, even when he is not speaking *ex cathedra*. That is, it must be shown in such a way that his supreme magisterium is acknowledged with reverence, the judgments made by him are sincerely adhered to, according to his manifest mind and will. His mind and will in the matter may be known chiefly either from the character of the documents, from his frequent repetition of the same doctrine, or from his manner of speaking. (Vat. II, *The Church*, 25)

The Pope— A Human Being Guided By the Holy Spirit

Many have a "hang-up" concerning the infallibility of the Supreme Pontiff because they say, "He is just a human being like us. He has faults and failings, and in the history of the Church we even had sinful Popes." Infallibility does not extend to the personal life of the Pope. He has temptations like all of us and he has the capability of falling into sin. He must work out his salvation, too. It is only when he is speaking as the Universal teacher of the Church on faith and morals that he enjoys infallibility, that is, when he is defining a doctrine *ex cathedra*. He is directly guided by the Holy Spirit, and if we are so foolish as to go contrary to his teachings we are rejecting the guidance and directives of the Holy Spirit.

Successors of Apostles—Bishops of the Church

In order to carry out the mission entrusted to them by Christ, the Apostles appointed successors in the Church.

> That divine mission, entrusted by Christ to the Apostles, will last until the end of the world (Mt. 28:20), since the Gospel which was to

be handed down by them is for all time the source of all life for the Church. For this reason the Apostles took care to appoint successors in this hierarchically structured society. (Vat. II, *The Church*, 20)

The successors of the Apostles are the bishops in the Church.

Continuing in the same task of clarification begun by Vatican I, this Council has decided to declare and proclaim before all men its teaching concerning bishops, the successors of the Apostles, who together with the successor of Peter, the Vicar of Christ and the Head of the whole visible Church, govern the house of the living God. (Vat. II, *The Church*, 18)

Just as the role that the Lord gave individually to Peter, the first among the Apostles, is permanent and was meant to be transmitted to his successors, so also the Apostles' office of nurturing the Church is permanent, and was meant to be exercised without interruption by the sacred order of bishops. Therefore, this sacred Synod teaches that by Divine institution bishops have succeeded to the place of the Apostles as shepherds of the Church, and that he who hears them, hears Christ, while he who rejects them, rejects Christ and Him who sent Christ. (Vat. II, *The Church*, 20)

A bishop is constituted a member of the episcopal body by sacramental consecration, and by hierarchical union with the head and members of the body.

... One is constituted a member of the episcopal body by virtue of sacramental consecration and by hierarchical communion with the head and members of the body. (Vat. II, *The Church*, 22)

The bishops do not enjoy the prerogative of infallibility; nevertheless they can proclaim Christ's doctrine infallibly.

Although the individual bishops do not enjoy the prerogative of infallibility, they can nevertheless proclaim Christ's doctrine infallibly. This is so, even when they are dispersed around the world, provided that while maintaining the bond of unity among themselves and with Peter's successor, and while teaching authentically on a matter of faith and morals, they concur in a single viewpoint as the one which must be held conclusively. This authority is even more clearly verified when, gathered together in an ecumenical council, they are teachers and judges of faith and morals for the universal Church. Their definitions must then be adhered to with the submission of faith.

The infallibility promised to the Church resides also in the body of bishops when that body exercises supreme teaching authority with the successor of Peter. (Vat. II, *The Church*, 25)

Ecumenical Council

The supreme teaching authority is exercised in a solemn way through an ecumenical council.

The supreme teaching authority with which this college is empowered over the whole Church is exercised in a solemn way through an ecumenical council. A council is never ecumenical unless it is confirmed or at least accepted as such by the successor of Peter. It is the prerogative of the Roman Pontiff to convoke these councils, to preside over them, and to confirm them. The same collegiate power can be exercised in union with the Pope by the bishops living in all parts of the world, provided that the head of the college calls them to collegiate action, or at least so approves or freely accepts the united actions of the dispersed bishops, that it is made a true collegiate act. (Vat. II, *The Church*, 22)

It is necessary that the Roman Pontiff convokes or confirms an ecumenical council because Christ made the Supreme Pontiff alone the rock and keybearer of the Church.

... Together with its head, the Roman Pontiff, and never without this head, the episcopal order is the subject of supreme and full power over the universal Church. But this power can be exercised only with the consent of the Roman Pontiff. For Our Lord made Simon Peter alone the rock and keybearer of the Church (cf. Mt. 16: 18-19), and appointed him shepherd of the whole flock. (cf. Jn. 21:15ff) (Vat. II, *The Church*, 22)

The collegial unity is apparent when the bishops act together with the Holy Father.

This collegial union is apparent also in the mutual relations of the individual bishops with particular churches and with the universal Church. The Roman Pontiff, as the successor of Peter, is the perpetual and visible source and foundation of the unity of the bishops and of the multitude of the faithful. The individual bishop, however, is the visible principle and foundation of unity in his particular church, fashioned after the model of the universal Church. In and from such individual churches there comes into being the one and only Catholic Church. For this reason each individual bishop represents his own church, but all of them together in union with the Pope represent the entire Church joined in the bond of peace, love and unity. (Vat. II, *The Church,* 23)

Duties of Bishops

The duties of the bishops are to teach, govern, and sanctify.

> But episcopal consecration, together with the office of sanctifying also confers the offices of teaching and of governing. (Those, however, of their very nature, can be exercised in hierarchical communion with the head and the members of the college.) For from tradition, which is expressed especially in liturgical rites and in the practice of the Church both of the East and of the West, it is clear that, by means of the imposition of hands and the words of consecration, the grace of the Holy Spirit is conferred, and the sacred character so impressed, that bishops in an eminent and visible way undertake Christ's own role as Teacher, Shepherd, and High Priest and that they act in His Person. (Vat. II, *The Church,* 21)

The bishop fulfills the office of teaching mainly by preaching the Gospels. He explains the faith that must be believed and put into practice. He fulfills his office of sanctifying through the liturgical service and the administration of the Sacraments. He governs the particular church entrusted to him by his council, exhortations, and examples as well as by his authority and sacred power. (Cf. Vat. II, *The Church,* 25, 26, 27)

The faithful should adhere to the teachings of the bishops with religious assent.

> In matters of faith and morals, the bishops speak in the name of Christ and the faithful are to accept their teaching and adhere to it with religious assent of soul. (Vat. II, *The Church,* 25)

The authority of the Roman Pontiff does not lessen or conflict with the bishops' authority, but it strengthens it.

The pastoral office or the habitual and daily care of their sheep is entrusted to them completely. Nor are they to be regarded as vicars of the Roman Pontiff, for they exercise an authority which is proper to them, and are quite correctly called 'prelates,' heads of the people whom they govern. Their power, therefore, is not destroyed by the supreme and universal power. On the contrary it is affirmed, strengthened and vindicated thereby, since the Holy Spirit unfailingly preserves the form of government established by Christ the Lord in His Church. (Vat. II, *The Church*, 27)

The Magisterium of the Church

The true teachings of the Church in regard to faith and morals come to us through the authentic teaching authority of the Magisterium of the Church, and from anyone who is teaching in complete accord with the Magisterium. Who are the official teachers in the Magisterium of the Church? Only the Pope and the Bishops. Then, what about the teachings of theologians, experts, and priests in religious matters? They are only advisors to the Magisterium of the Church. If they express their own opinions contrary to what the Magisterium of the Church teaches, then these are not the teachings of the Church. The People of God would be foolish to follow and accept their teaching. It is important that we realize this, and that we study and know what the true teachings of the Magisterium of the Church are.

Episcopal Conferences

Regional episcopal conferences are held at various times throughout the year. At these conferences, the bishops are able to dialogue about matters which pertain to the well-being of the Church in their areas. They are able to learn from one another what action should be taken so that they can teach, govern, and sanctify the People of God under their jurisdiction, and how best to aid the communities in which they find themselves.

National episcopal conferences are held once or twice a year. These conferences are important because they create a bond of unity among the bishops. It helps them to keep up with what is going on in the Church, the nation, and the world. It helps them to set policies that should be enacted for the benefit of mankind. Also more force is given to the pronouncements made at these conferences on various world issues because the bishops are speaking as a corporate body.

Various commissions are established by the National Episcopal conferences and they report back to the bishops. This is a great help to the bishops in formulating their policies.

The delegates to the bishops' synod are also chosen at these bishops' conferences. The delegates are able to know what the bishops are thinking. They can take their knowledge and experience to the synod's meeting in Rome, and thus be in a better position to advise the Holy Father.

The Bishops' Synod

The bishops' synod is only an advisory body. It has an agenda of topics to be discussed concerning Church and world matters. The recommendations they make should be made for the good of the Church and in accord with the Will of God. The Holy Father has the right to accept or reject any recommendation made by the bishops' synod.

The Bishop—A Shepherd

The bishop is to be a shepherd to all who are under him. He is to be a leader; willing to listen, to guide, and to counsel. He should love his people and take care of them through his prayer, preaching, and works of charity. The day is past when he was considered "Lord and Master." Rather, he is to be a man of service. He should exemplify the virtues of Christ in his ministry. He should be Christlike in all his dealings with the People of God.

We can readily see that the office of the bishop is a tremendous one, and we should gladly support him by our cooperation and prayers. If this is true of the bishop, it is more true of the Holy Father, whom we should also love, respect, and obey.

The Ministerial Priesthood

The bishop cannot do his work effectively or fulfill his mission without the help of associates in the ministry. That is why the Church has established the ministerial priesthood. The priest is one who has been called by God and set aside to carry out the things that pertain to God.

> Although priests do not possess the highest degree of the priesthood, and although they are dependent on the bishops in the exercise of their power, they are nevertheless united with the bishops in sacerdotal dignity, by the power of the Sacrament of Orders, and in the image of Christ the eternal High Priest (Heb. 5: 1-10; 7:24; 9:11-28), they are consecrated to preach the Gospel, shepherd the faithful, and celebrate Divine Worship as true priests of the New Testament. Partakers of the function of Christ the sole mediator (1 Tim. 2:5) on their level of ministry, they announce the Divine Word to all. (Vat. II, *The Church*, 28)

The priest is to represent the bishop in the local individual congregations of the faithful.

> Associated with their bishop in a spirit of trust and generosity, priests make him present in a certain sense in the individual local congregations of the faithful, and take upon themselves, as far as they are able, his duties and concerns, discharging them with daily care.... Intent always upon the welfare of God's children, they must strive to lend their efforts to the personal work of the whole diocese, and even of the entire Church. (Vat. II *The Church*, 28)

Duties of the Priest

The priest is to offer liturgical service, administer the Sacraments, preach the Gospel, lead and serve the local community so that the entire people may in fact be distinguished as the Church of God.

> Exercising within the limits of their authority the function of Christ as Shepherd and Head, they gather together God's family as a brotherhood all of one mind and lead them in the Spirit, through Christ, to God the Father. In the midst of the flock they adore Him in Spirit and truth (cf. Jn. 4:24). Finally they labor in word and doctrine (cf. 1 Tim. 5:17), believing what they have read and meditated upon in the law of the Lord, teaching what they believe, and practicing what they teach. (Vat. II, *The Church*, 28)

Priests should work in harmony with the bishop and the Holy

Father so that unity may prevail. They should love, respect and obey them. In other words they, too, should be Christlike towards the bishop and Holy Father and the people with whom they work.

> Because the human race today is joining more and more into a civic, economic, and social unity, it is that much more necessary that priests, united in concern and effort, under the leadership of the bishops and the Supreme Pontiff, wipe out every kind of division, so that the whole human race may be brought into the unity of the Family of God. (Vat. II, *The Church*, 28)

Priests' Synod

One way in which this can be accomplished is the priests' synod. This synod should be an effective body to advise the bishop of the problems of the diocese, to make recommendations on how to better fulfill the ministry, and to build up the Church. It should strive to show ways and means to better implement the policies of the diocese and the Church for the well being of the People of God.

The priests' synod should make every effort to give an opportunity to all priests, sisters, brothers, seminarians, those aspiring to religious life, to express their views, opinions, and recommendations on every important issue which affects the Church, the diocese, and the community. The views of the lay people can be obtained through parish councils. All this material should be synthesized so that an agenda can be drawn up for the meeting of the priests' synod, which should be held once or twice a year.

The priests' synod is also only an advisory body. It is important that the advice given to the bishop be a true representation of the thinking of the whole diocese, and not just their own ideas or pet projects. It would be well to have representatives present at the meetings, that is, other priests, brothers, sisters, lay people, and seminarians. The bishop, too, should be there to listen and watch the proceedings. However, he should not interfere so that the work of the synod may be effective. Nevertheless, he has the right to accept or reject the advice, which he is to do only after deliberation. He always has to keep in mind what is best for the Church, the diocese, the community.

The priest's role is essential in the Church, in the diocese, and in the community and that is why it is so sad when any priest abandons his mission. He more than anyone else can help the People of God to fulfill their commitment, to grow in the spiritual life to develop to maturity. Why is this true? Because he is with the People of God more than anyone else. The priest has a great mission, which can never be taken lightly, because it has eternal consequences. Thus, we can see the importance of praying for him.

Deaconate

Just as the bishop cannot fulfill his mission without the help of the priest, so the priest cannot fulfill his mission without the help of others. He needs the assistance of lay people and sometimes a deacon. The deacon can aid the priest in the ministry of service.

> At a lower level of the hierarchy are deacons, upon whose hands are imposed 'Not unto the priesthood, but unto a ministry of service.' For strengthened by sacramental grace, in communion with the bishop and his group of priests, they serve the People of God in the ministry of the liturgy, of the word, and of Charity. (Vat. II, *The Church*, 29)

The duties of the deacon are to solemnly administer baptism, to be a dispenser and custodian of the Eucharist, to bless marriages in the name of the Church, to preach and instruct the faithful, to assist the dying and console the sick, to officiate at funerals and burial services. A deacon can perform most of the duties of the priest except offering Mass, forgiving sin, and giving the Last Sacraments. He should be the right hand of the priest as the priest is of the bishop.

Thus the hierarchical Church intended by Christ and established by the Apostles has come down to us through the centuries and is present with us today. In this time of confusion and unrest we should remember the history of the Church serving people like us. The Apostles dispersed after Pentecost to various countries of the world to preach the Gospel of Jesus Christ. They baptized, set up authority, and inspired thousands to follow the Messiah.

Most often they died in a distant land, persecuted and martyred for the faith. As they died, or as they finished their ministries in one land, they would give authority to bishops and priests to continue the good works.

The Growth of The Church

In this way the Church grew in the Roman Empire, and the sight of converts to the faith alarmed the Romans. Slaves and freemen were welcome in the Church, as well as noble Roman families, and this threatened the heart of Rome, which was based on slavery and on a caste system. Tiberius, the Emperor who was on the throne when Christ was crucified, was the first to voice distrust and apprehension about the Church. His nephew, Caligula, who followed Tiberius to the throne, was the first to order open persecution. Then the ordeals in the arenas began. Emperors like Nero and Diocletian condemned more than two million Christians to death. They persecuted the Christians to defend the Rome they knew. Thousands died when the Emperors became bored or feared that the starvation in the city might cause civil riots. Christians were torn to pieces to provide amusement for the Roman citizens, and to take their minds off their empty stomachs.

The more persecutions, however, the greater the spread of Christianity. As Tertullian observed: "The blood of martyrs is the seed of Christianity." The blessed martyrs died in the horrors of torture pits or as a blazing torch for Roman banquets, but they died giving praise to Christ or holding silence in the face of torment and fear.

The Edict of Milan, issued in 313 A.D., brought peace to the Church. Emperor Constantine had been converted through a miraculous vision while on the battlefield, and he established Christianity as the state religion of Rome. Within sixty years, however, thousands again faced torture and death for the Faith. The Huns and Vandals and other barbarian tribes ravaged the whole of Europe and conquered even Rome. The Dark Ages came upon the civilized western world, and only the Church kept the light of culture, truth, and faith alive. Monks and nuns in silent monasteries worked and studied and prayed and kept the ancient ways of Rome and Greece alive in writings, in art, in sculpture.

At the same time, the Church sent out missionaries to preach to other barbaric tribes. St. Augustine went to England to convert that island. St. Patrick won the people of Ireland. St. Boniface turned the wild tribesmen of Germany into Christians. Spain and France followed the Sign of the Cross soon after, and the Church was one—with one baptism, one faith, one Blessed Lord.

Islam rose out of the East to bring more agony to the Church in the eighth century. Spain and France fell before the invincible Mohammedan armies, and even Rome was sacked by their legions. The Fall of Jerusalem brought more grief to Christendom and inspired men to display the Cross of Christ on their garments and to move across the world in crusades.

When the crusades ended, the renaissance of Europe began, and the time of schisms and heresies started for the Church. Religious wars and feuds kept the nations apart or divided until the sixteenth century, when the reformation tore the Church asunder. Yet, the Church emerged from this period stronger and purified. At the same time her missionaries were crossing to the new world, where lands were being conquered and souls were being left untrained and unloved.

Today, as in the past, the Church is actively at work in every nation on earth. There are nations which have silenced the Church outwardly and have imprisoned her prelates and priests, but the work continues in the blood of martyrs. The work of the Church is never ended, because the Church is universal, and when one part bleeds and dies, another takes up and prays, making atonement. At present the Church has more than 550,000,000 members in all parts of the world. There are more than 450,000 priests, 2,500 prelates, and one head, the Pope. In the foreign missions, in those areas where the Church has always followed Christ's explicit command to preach the Gospel, the Church has 35,000 priests, 15,000 lay brothers and 70,000 sisters.

Today, as in the early days when Christians were being hounded and beaten for their faith, the Church continues the specific tasks assigned to Her by Christ. The Church continues His teachings and example, applying the merits of His Sacrifice on the Cross to all men until the end of the world.

The second dimension of the Pilgrim Church is the faithful, who also constitute the People of God. The hierarchy and the faithful are not meant to be two separate camps in opposition to each other; but they are to complement one another so that we have one Church. The hierarchy and the faithful have the privilege and duty to work together in service for the extension of the Kingdom of God on earth. They are to fulfill their respective missions in charity and unity for the well-being of all mankind.

Rapid Changes in World

Today we are living in a new age where rapid changes are spreading across the world. These changes were brought about by man's intelligence and creative ability and they have done much for the progress of man on earth. We see the world advancing toward unification of all mankind through communication, through scientific discoveries, through technological and economic advances. All this progress contributes toward a better society and helps mankind fulfill its mission, given by God, to subdue the earth.

Changes Caused Confusion

Whenever there are changes, and especially when there is a rapid evolution, many doubts, uncertainties, and difficulties arise. In our world, it seems that we have our share of all these because life, liberty, and human dignity are everywhere threatened. Many men are crushed by oppressive rulers, or by their own egoism, selfishness, greed, or indifference. Wherever we look we can see social injustice, a disproportion between the rich and the poor, illiteracy and ignorance, children being abandoned, the life of the unborn being snuffed out, and seemingly endless wars.

Searching For Identity

Modern man feels threatened and fearful because he is overwhelmed by the complex situation in which he finds himself. He is no longer able to discern permanent values, or to harmonize them with recent discoveries. One of the main reasons for this is that he does not have God in his life, or he has rejected God. Therefore he has lost the real meaning of life and he is searching for his identity. This can be a most painful experience for man because he questions everything in his life, in society, even the relevancy of religion.

Social Injustice—Impact on Christianity

Modern man, in large numbers, is contesting the type of society we know. He thinks that society does not have sufficient justice, but is filled with inequalities and with new forms of slavery; that society does not have enough fraternal charity, but is filled with hate, class warfare, and racial discrimination, that the world does not work for the development of the whole man, but places more value on material and technological progress. He also feels that the world is not open enough to new values, but withdraws itself within its own structures.

These conditions have a tremendous impact upon Christians and their way of life. Some are led to a deeper commitment to Christ and to service in the Church because superstitious and magical concepts have been cleansed from their outlook on life and religion. They are able to make a more personal adherence to faith.

On the other hand, large numbers are separating themselves from religion and religious practices. Many opt for this mode of living because they think that it is necessary for scientific progress or a new form of humanism.

Thus, there are some who lose their confidence in the Church and consider her no longer an instrument of salvation, or a sign working among nations. They feel that the Church is unfaithful to Christ, that it is incapable of answering the spiritual needs of today, and has outlived its usefulness.

Some are not able to harmonize the historical and traditional forms on the one hand, and the requirements of the modern world on the other. Yet, we are men of this world and we must live in it. We must learn how to be a true Christian witness to the world.

True Christian Witness to the World

To be true witnesses as Christians we have to put on a new mind and convert ourselves without ceasing. We have to abandon false idols to serve the one true and living God. (1 Thess. 1: 9-10), renewing ourselves by a spiritual transformation (Eph. 4: 20-24).

> Do not be conformed to this world but be transformed by the renewal of your mind, that you may prove what is the Will of God, what is good and acceptable and perfect. (Rom. 12.2)
> To renew spiritually is, first of all, to place yourself in the Presence of Christ, Who calls on each individual to meet Him, to follow Him, to serve Him in others. It means recognizing the goodness of God in the total action of your daily life. It means understanding that your vocation is a vocation to love, that you must reveal and announce yourself. It means intensifying your effort to be present to the men of today, trying to see them through the eyes of Christ. It means, finally, communicating the life of the Church, making your own 'its initiatives and intentions—' (SS.CC. Rule of Life, 17)

To renew ourselves we have to continually revise the plan governing our lives. We all know that tradition, habit, customs, and past history influence our lives. Yet, today, the young especially want freedom of their own. They want self-determination, even if it deprives them of precious heritages. Everyone is influenced by contemporary appeal, that is, environment, fashion, and the outside world. This influence is extremely strong and tends to reduce man to one type, to a common moral stature, to an impersonal democracy. Young people are especially vulnerable and they are swept along with the multitude, becoming an anonymous number.

Faithfulness to Jesus Christ and Individual Personality

The question arises, can man, overwhelmed by present conditions in the world, defend, keep, and promote a personality of his own in faithfulness to his model, Jesus Christ?

The influence of authority is also being rejected because it is looked upon as restricting freedom, both personal or collective.

Yet authority is more indispensable than ever in a society as complex as ours.

Thus again the question arises, can man be faithful to Christ and still promote, defend, and keep a personality of his own?

Live by The Spirit

A real authentic Christian character can be formed if we but follow the advice of St. Paul: "Since we live by the Spirit, let us be directed by the Spirit" (Gal. 5:25).

To show the meaning of these words of St. Paul we will quote from Pope Paul's talk on "The Christian Life Demands Consistency":

> We cannot give here the exegesis of a proposal in which a great part of the Apostle's doctrine is condensed. We will just say that while it releases from observance of the legality characteristic of the Old Testament, it transfers the root of moral life, as Christ did in the Gospel and particularly in the Sermon on the Mount, inside man, let us even say (subject to completing these terms with the relative due explanations) to conscience, to the freedom of the human person.
>
> And we must ask ourselves at once: What does it mean 'to live by the Spirit?' Here there opens the theology of Christian life, which cannot be conceived outside the plan of salvation installed by Christ: Our life is not an isolated phenomenon, it is not a fact that is an end in itself. It is an existence called to an extraordinary destiny, which transcends it and envelops it at the same time, to which we can and must adhere by means of an essential act, which is called faith. And faith puts us into the circle of a vital Divine communication which is called grace, and grace is the action of the Holy Spirit in us; it is the participation in Divine life (Cf. Lagrange, *Epitre aux Galates*, p. 147). All this presupposes a magisterium and a ministry; the Church offers them to us, and makes it possible for us 'to live by the Spirit.' This is the authentic principle of Christian life.

One thing is certain: life needs principles. A really human philosophy is necessary and above that there must shine the light of faith. Without principles and faith a man walks in the shadow of darkness, doubt, skepticism, and despair. The confusion and revolution in the modern world are due to a lack of true, strong, and fertile principles. For the most part, modern man's faith is weak or even non-existent. But the Christian has both principles and faith; thus he should be a consistent man, a man of character, a righteous man. Therefore we have a challenge today—Christian be a Christian! He can do this if he is guided by the Holy Spirit.

This glorious hope is not illusory; this state of mind is not a beautiful dream induced by wishful thinking. St. Paul points to the gift of the Holy Spirit whom the Father (and the Son) bestowed upon each Christian in baptism (cf. Rom. 5:1-5). The Spirit's Presence, His dynamic and sanctifying activity, in the life of the believer, manifests God's mercy and is a sure pledge of mercies to come. The Christian has to persevere in faith, hope, and charity to the end.

> The love of God (for us) has been poured into our hearts by the Holy Spirit Who has been given to us. (Rom. 5:5)

These words should be comforting in light of parallel passages; it asserts that the Christian shares in the life of the Trinity through sanctifying grace.

At the Last Supper, Christ said, "I have many things to say to you but you cannot bear them now—but when He, the Spirit of truth, has come, He will guide you into the whole truth." (cf. Jn. 16:12-15).

Guidance of Holy Spirit

The word "guide" frequently occurs in the Greek Old Testament, in connection with God's dealings with Israel. God guided Israel by a pillar of cloud by day and of fire by night (Numb. 24:8; Deut. 1:33). In the Psalms the same word is used in reference to the guidance of an individual's life (Ps. 5:8; 24:5.9; 30:3; 137:24). These passages assume the presence in human life of a Divine guide. The guide and teacher of the New Israel and of its individual members is the Holy Spirit.

The Holy Spirit guides the Church and Her members to the whole truth about Jesus Christ and the Gospels. He teaches nothing but what He Himself has received from the Father through the Son. The Holy Spirit is ever receiving and imparting what He receives: not a new revelation, but new insights into the revelations of Jesus Christ—the doctrine, the Mass, the Sacraments, the life of the Body of Christ.

The Revealed Truths of The Blessed Trinity

Each new insight that the Holy Spirit will give is a fresh glorification of Christ, and an enlargement of man's sense of His nature, His work, His unsearchable riches so that men will come to know that "Christ is everything in each of them" (Col. 3:11). As the Son glorified the Father on earth, the Holy Spirit glorifies the Son. The Father is the source of the revelation communicated to men by the Son, and the Holy Spirit brings it to completion, who in this way glorifies both the Son and the Father. There are not three revelations, but *one*.

We give glory to the Triune God by believing and living the sanctifying and saving truths that have been revealed. We can know from reason that God is in His creatures in a threefold manner: by His Power, since all creatures are subject to His dominion; by His Wisdom, because He sees all, even our most secret thoughts; by His Essence, since He acts everywhere sustaining all things in being. But, Revelation has told us much more. Through the recreation of human nature wrought by the Trinity many and precious treasures are ours. The greatest is life, abundant life, together with Uncreated Grace or God Himself. God by grace abides in us as in a temple, in an intimate and singular manner.

> Know you not that your body is the temple of the Holy Spirit who is within you? (1 Cor. 3:16; 6:19; cf. Rom. 8:8; 11 Cor. 13:5; Eph. 3:17; 11 Tim. 1:14; St. James 4:5)

We may give glory to the Three Persons of the Adorable Trinity all the day long, by thinking, speaking, and acting as children of the Father, as brethren and members of the well-beloved Son, as temples of the Spirit of Truth and Sanctifier of our souls.

Ordinary Activity of the Holy Spirit in the Church

On the day of Pentecost, the Holy Spirit came to abide with

and in the Church, with and in each member of the Mystical Body of Christ, energizing, purifying, enlightening, protecting, and strengthening the Body of Christ and His members. This was the ordinary activity of the Holy Spirit in the Church, as we can see from what is related in the Acts of the Apostles, for the first thirty years of the Church's existence. Since then, down through the centuries, this has been the ordinary activity of the Holy Spirit in Her and in Her members.

Sevenfold Gifts of the Holy Spirit

When we put on Christ, that is, when we have been given a share in the Divine Nature and life at baptism, the Holy Spirit comes to dwell in us with His sevenfold gifts. These are infused supernatural habits, by which we are able to respond more readily, more generously, and more fruitfully to His inspirations within us.

Three of the gifts of the Holy Spirit are meant to aid and perfect the virtue of faith, the theological virtue which inclines our mind under the influence of the will to assent to the truths revealed by God, who can neither deceive or be deceived because He is truth itself. Faith places before us a sublime goal: an eternal life of happiness with God, the angels, and the saints. It places before us the means to achieve that sublime goal, a life of union with God here on earth.

Yet, faith is an imperfect virtue by its very nature. It does not reveal God to us immediately, but only obscurely, as "Through a glass in a dark manner" (1 Cor. 13:12). We can form only a mental picture of God from affirmative and negative statements. God is this or that; God is not this or that; He does this or that, or He doesn't do this or that.

Because faith is essentially obscure it needs the gifts of the Holy Spirit to perfect it. We need the perfecting influence of the three gifts of the Holy Spirit because by faith we give assent to three entirely different kinds of revealed truths.

Gift of Wisdom

The *gift of wisdom,* an intellectual gift, perfects the virtue of faith by enlightening the mind concerning the primary truths of Divine revelation, that is, the mysteries properly so called. We could never come to the knowledge of these mysteries by our own reasoning powers. For example, the mystery of the Blessed Trinity, the redemptive Incarnation, or the Real Presence of Christ in the Eucharist.

The Holy Spirit is moved to activate the gift of wisdom in a particular soul in proportion to the soul's exercise of the virtue of charity. Charity is that virtue which causes us to love God above all things, and to love our neighbor for the love of God. God has made our love of neighbor the test of our love for Him. Thus the gift of wisdom "formally" resides in our intellect and "effectively" in our will as perfected by charity. Thus the gift of wisdom accidentally perfects the virtue of charity. The knowledge of the mysteries of faith tends to increase charity in the soul. This, in turn, moves the Holy Spirit to give the soul even more knowledge of these mysteries. The process goes on and on, moving the soul upward to God.

Gift of Understanding

The *gift of understanding* perfects the virtue of faith by throwing light upon the secondary truths of faith, that is, natural truths, which human reason radically can know of itself but needs the aid of this gift to understand them correctly. We are speaking here of ultimate truths in the natural order, dealing with God's nature and our relationship with Him. These truths really are in the field of philosophy, mainly metaphysics.

The Holy Spirit is moved to activate this gift in a particular soul to further enlighten the mind on these ultimate natural truths to perfect the virtue of hope. The Holy Spirit gives this gift in proportion as the soul exercises the virtue of hope. Hope is the virtue which gives us the desire to possess God as our highest good, and we expect with a firm confidence that we will possess Him eternally. The activation of the gift of understanding accidentally perfects the virtue of hope, but primarily the virtue of faith. The gift of understanding makes us better understand God's power and mercy.

Gift of Knowledge

The *gift of knowledge* perfects the virtue of faith by throwing light on tertiary truths, that is, proximate truths. These truths have to do with creatures, mainly man, individually and socially. "The gift of knowledge is only about human or created things" (St. Thomas 11-11, q. 9, a. 2); for example, that man is a composite of body and soul, that the intellect can attain truth with certitude, that the human will is free. Human reason can discover these truths for itself. These truths usually fall within the scope of philosophy of nature.

The Holy Spirit is moved to activate this gift in a particular soul in proportion to the soul's exercise of the virtue of fear. The virtue of fear restrains man from the evil use of creatures because of God's infinite justice and punishment of sin. The struggle of the soul to avoid sin moves the Holy Spirit to activate this gift. As St. Thomas says, the gift of knowledge "makes us know experimentally the emptiness of created things, all that is defectible and deficient in them and in ourselves" (11-11, q.9, a.4). The gift of knowledge perfects the virtue of faith, and "formally" resides in the intellect, but also in the will "effectively" as perfected by the virtue of fear.

As in the case of wisdom and charity, understanding and hope, the gift of knowledge accidentally perfects the virtue of fear. As the virtue of fear increases, the Holy Spirit gives the soul a more penetrating knowledge and estimation of creatures at their true value.

Some may ask, why did God reveal secondary and proximate truths to us if we can know them by the use of our natural reason?

> It is owing to this Divine revelation, assuredly, that even in the present condition of the human race, those religious truths which are by their very nature accessible to human reason can easily be known by all men with solid certitude and with no trace of error. Nevertheless, it must not be argued that the revelation (of these natural truths) is, for that reason, absolutely necessary. It is necessary only because God, out of His infinite goodness, destined man to a supernatural end, that is, to a participation in the good things of God, which altogether exceed the human mental grasp; for 'eye has not seen, nor ear heard, nor has it

entered into the heart of man, what things God has prepared for those who love Him' (1 Cor. 2:9). (Vat. I Const, *The Catholic Faith*, Chapter 2)

All three gifts perfect the virtue of faith and "formally" reside in the intellect: in the speculative intellect, which seeks truth, and in the practical intellect which ordains truth to action. Faith in the speculative sense means that we give firm assent to truths revealed by God, Who cannot deceive or be deceived, and in the practical sense—that we carry out what we believe in action—in works.

> Faith consists primarily and principally in speculation, inasmuch as it (faith) is founded on the First Truth (God), is also the last and for the sake of which our works are done; hence it is that faith extends to works. (St. Thomas, 11-11, q. 9, a.3)

The other four gifts of the Holy Spirit perfect the virtues of prudence, justice, fortitude, and temperance, which we call moral virtues.

Gift of Counsel

The *gift of counsel* perfects the exercise of the moral virtue of prudence. The virtue of prudence inclines our intellect to choose the best means to obtain our goals, by subordinating them to our true ultimate end, the beatific vision of God. In exercising the virtue of prudence, we examine the situation before us, trying to see what is best in this circumstance so that we may judge correctly in carrying out our actions. We may even have to seek advice in more serious cases so that we may act rightly.

The gift of counsel perfects the moral virtue of prudence by helping us to do promptly and correctly, as by a supernatural instinct, what we should do here and now. The Holy Spirit guides us in an instant to make the correct choice, even in the most difficult circumstances.

Gift of Piety

The *gift of piety* perfects the virtue of religion, and through it the virtue of justice. The moral virtue of justice inclines our will to render what is due to others at all times. This covers a wide range of human relations. It also includes the virtue of religion whereby we render to God what is His due.

The gift of piety begets in us, in our will, a filial commitment to God as the beginning and end of our supernatural life. It helps to fulfill our religious duties promptly and with joy. Through it the Holy Spirit also transforms our duties of justice toward our fellowmen.

Gift of Fortitude

The *gift of fortitude* perfects the virtue of fortitude by sustaining our courage in the face of great obstacles, by helping us to undertake great tasks and endure great trials. The virtue of fortitude strengthens the will not to deviate from the path of pursuing difficult goals. It helps us to endure misfortunes even for a long time. The gift of fortitude fortifies this virtue and makes it operative.

Gift of Fear

The *gift of fear* perfects the virtue of temperance, which controls and directs our desires for earthly pleasure, especially sense pleasure. The gift of fear induces the soul to have filial fear, that is, profound reverence for God, and it grows with the progress of charity. It is different from servile fear, which fears God's justice and His punishment for sin. Although one never is free from this type of fear, it diminishes in proportion to the growth of charity within the soul.

The gifts of the Holy Spirit perfect the theological and moral virtues in our spiritual life. The virtues and gifts perfect a human being by perfecting his two distinctive human powers: his intellect and his will. Each gift and each virtue has repercussions on all others in the actual living of our spiritual life so we cannot really consider them as separate, and only operative in their own separate unit or sphere; even if each one perfects the human powers in their own special way.

The soul practices the virtues, and to the extent that it does, it overcomes its evil inclination and sin, thus freeing itself so that it is able to give itself to God. To that extent that it does so, the Holy Spirit moves in and operates in the soul, but only with the soul freely consenting to His action.

Extraordinary Activity of Holy Spirit in Spiritual Life

However, there are, at times, some privileged souls in whom the Holy Spirit works in a special manner. He gives extraordinary graces and gifts. This may be from childhood, for example, the Little Flower or Dominic Savio; or in the cases of others they make rapid progress in the spiritual life without the proportionate perfection of the virtues. This is an exception granted through the power of the Holy Spirit. Usually the development and perfection of the spiritual life is a gradual one. We have to learn to be patient and open to the Spirit at all times if we want to develop our spiritual life correctly. God the Holy Spirit acts in us. It is He who inspires our actions.

God acts in us through love. He offers us genuine friendship. The Apostles spoke of it again and again with joy:

> For you have not received the spirit of bondage again in fear: but you have received the spirit of adoption of sons, whereby we cry Abba (Father). For the Spirit himself gives testimony to our spirit that we are the sons of God. (Rom. 8:15-16)

This new life, this redemption, must be understood for what it is. It is not a fiction, not a pretense at living with God, but actually a new life.

> Unless a man be born again of water and the Holy Spirit ... By the laver of regeneration and renovation of the Holy Spirit he has regenerated us into a lively hope ... by his own will he has gotten us by the Word of Truth. (John 3:5)

Union With God—Goal of Life

Read what St. Bonaventure declares possible for those who were redeemed by Christ:

This is the highest perfection of man in this life, so to live in God that the whole soul with all her powers and forces united in God, becomes one spirit with Him. Also that she thinks of nothing but God... For the image of God in the soul consists in three powers ... She must be imprinted with Him as wax in the seal. And this never happens perfectly but when the understanding is perfectly enlightened in the knowledge of God, who is the Supreme Truth; the will perfectly moved to love the supreme Goodness, and the memory perfectly absorbed in beholding, enjoying and holding the Beatitude ...

There does the soul truly rest; there she perfects herself in the clearness of light, the greatness of the divine blessedness, and the security of Peace.

Most of us will never reach such a state of spiritual development, because we have not been taught or inspired to live in such a manner. Perhaps it is no longer possible for most people to glimpse life in this way.

Why is this true for many? Because man has the gift of free will, he can choose good or evil for himself, he is subject to error and to the daily struggle for mastery over himself. The reason for this is that we so often mistake something as being good for us, when actually it contains the seed of death in it. We are so vulnerable to the soft words of others, to the seemingly good intentions, to the flattery they offer us. We also seek to be loved by others, to be considered good, to appear respectable. How many times do we deceive ourselves into thinking that we are right, when actually we are seeking ourselves or our own glory?

Thousands of us live half-lives, shadowy existences somewhere between the light of God and the total darkness of the beast. Our senses delight in color, sound, light, aromas and every other form of stimulation, and we cannot get enough of variety. We play mental games to protect our vanities and seek insane models for imitation.

If you wonder about this, ask yourself how many of your friends or neighbors delight in monthly copies of movie fan magazines or true confession types or playboy materials. Look about you and see that most people idolize anyone on television and believe every idiotic remark made by someone with a weekly show.

Intellectually we are also hindered. We do not think clearly and often make very poor decisions in even the simplest matters of daily life. Only the grace of the Redemption, through the Holy Spirit, can give us the ability to rise above ourselves and contemplate the ultimate sublime reality.

We are all called to personal holiness and to salvation. It is the action of the Holy Spirit within us that will deliver us from apathy and help us become true followers of Christ. It is the Holy Spirit who will bring us to live, act, and move in the Presence of God.

LIVING IN THE PRESENCE OF GOD

How many times have you been lonely, neglected, afraid, and abandoned? How many times have you felt that if you disappeared from the face of the earth, no one would notice or even mention it? You are a human being. You are one of the members of mankind, and we are all buffeted and frightened by the singleness of ourselves and the unity of others. We grasp, in some intuitive sense, what Pope Paul said about the Church and ourselves being in a two-fold time dimension. We are here and now, and yet we seem to understand that we were really made for a tomorrow in Paradise. This is where the alienation and the anxiety begin.

Let us seek to join our tomorrow and our present, in the way that the saints did when they lived on earth. It is a simple matter actually, suggested and perfected by a simple lay brother called Lawrence. He called it The Practice of the Presence of God.

Never Alone

When you are alone, you perhaps do things or fail to do things that you would never do in front of others. We are all like that. We call it relaxing alone. We call it taking time for ourselves. We humans do need a certain privacy, a certain intimacy with ourselves that allows us to put aside the cares and poses of everyday life. Actually, however, this state of aloneness, this privacy, is not true or possible.

> As St. Paul reminds us (1 Cor. 6:19), we are 'not our own.' We belong entirely to Christ. His Spirit has taken possession of us at Baptism. We are the Temples of the Holy Spirit. Our thoughts, our actions, our desires, are by rights more his than our own. (Thomas Merton, *Life and Holiness,* p. 12)

Think of it. When you are at the movie theatres, the drive-ins, watching TV, sleeping in bed, dining at a restaurant, praying in Church—you are not alone. You are in the Presence of the Triune God before Whom the angels prostrate and the heavens give praise and adoration. You dare to quarrel with others, swear, curse, tell vile stories or worse in the Presence of God.

The ancient Jews refused to write the name Yahweh. Yahweh meant He that is. Some Orthodox Jews still write Y....H in their letters or scrolls because they feel unworthy of uttering the Divine Name. We use the Name of God to curse our enemies or to accentuate our anger in a sentence!

Turn yourself around, then, to realize the strange contradiction which this world has caused in us all. Discover that you are the one who should be prostrate before God, singing His praises. And then be prepared for the wondrous change which can come about in your life.

Practice the Presence of God! This means that upon waking you will realize the awesome privilege which is yours in partaking of God's life. This will mean that you will at last recognize the fact that you are no longer alone, no longer abandoned. You will rise from your bed to offer yourself, without pose, without pride, and He will accept you within His Sacred Heart.

The practice of the Presence of God is more than just pious mutterings when you remember God. It is a turning inward and a turning outward at the same instant. You will lose sight of the old goals and discover new ones. You will learn the beautiful custom of forgetting people when they are not with you and learning to give praise.

Praise of Glory

Sister Elizabeth of the Trinity, a Carmelite cloistered nun who was a contemporary of the Little Flower, developed this way of life into a practice of perfection. She realized that we were made to give God praise in eternity and began the praise here. *Laudem Gloriae* is the title of her understanding, and one forgives her bad Latin when one understands the significance of the truth which she glimpsed. If our eternity will be spent, in the company of the angels and saints, in giving praise to God, why deprive ourselves of that wonderful privilege here and now? Why not begin Praise of Glory now?

This means placing ourselves in a particular condition mentally and spiritually. This means understanding what St. Denis calls the "Cloud of Unknowing" and the "Cloud of Forgetfulness." What do these terms signify? Our attempts to understand God are met with a Cloud of Unknowing, in that we are limited and we are finite, mortal creatures who are not too bright even about life, let alone about the Source of Life. We therefore have to understand that we will be groping our way to God for most of our lives ... living the Life of Faith. Thomas Merton describes faith as "not merely acquiescence of the mind in certain truths, it is the gift of our whole being to Truth Itself, to the Word of God."

Interior Recollection

At the same instant, we are obliged to detach ourselves from those who put obstacles in our paths. This means the Cloud of Forgetfulness. Or, in other words, we have to learn to practice interior recollection. Interior recollection is something that the saints and mystics understood as vital for anyone who would reach a certain degree of holiness. With our modern civilization pressing down on us from all sides, we are beginning to understand that interior recollection, quiet prayer, and meditation, are essential to us for sanity. We cannot give to others something that we do not possess in ourselves.

The Practice of the Presence of God is no more than a turning of oneself away from the thoughts of others or things on a continual basis. When you finish with a task or a conversation, forget it and give praise to God. When you are busy with some chore, offer it to God for His Glory. It will never matter what size or importance the chore. Do whatever you have to do in your state in life as an act of love and adoration for God and you will discover peace and contentment and courage. This was the Secret of the Little Flower, and look what a great saint she became.

Put the worries and cares that you have away from you. This does not mean that you enter a silly world of fantasy. Trust in God, rely on His Providence, and spend time giving Him praise and glory rather than fretting about that which you cannot help. This will bring about a rather startling change in you, you will discover. When the time comes for you to concentrate on a problem or to bring your resources to bear, you will discover that you have greater strength, greater resources. God is a simple being, not composed of three levels of existence. It is necessary to unify our beings, our composites. St. Thomas Aquinas said: "Only complicated unity on our part can mirror the Divine Simplicity of God." This means that we must have every one of our faculties under control and ready to move swiftly and easily into a given situation. Our loves must be rooted in the time dimensions that Pope Paul speaks of: we must be ready to translate tomorrow's promises into the activities of today. This must be habitual, not something that we must ponder and discuss and debate each day of our lives.

Turning to God Always—Being Tuned In!

We must learn to turn to God at every possible opportunity. When you are waiting in a doctor's office, or when waiting for a bus or a train—take the time to withdraw into the temple of your soul. When on a walk or a ride alone, put aside the radios and tapes and let the heart respond to the longings for union with God. When in Church listen for the first time and ponder the mystery of Him who waits in the tabernacle in silent love.

The model for this habitual living in the Presence of God is Mary, Our Mother, and the Mother of Christ. We should ask her aid.

> Mary became the Mother of God at the moment of the Incarnation. It was a moment for which God had richly prepared her. Through the fullness of grace which He gave her, Mary had lived a life of obedience to the Will of God. Her every thought and action had been formed in the burning crucible of charity or the love of God. (Thomas Aquinas, *My Way of Life*, Summa Theologica, Pt. 3, 11:7)

The practice of the Presence of God slowly forms the human being and reconstructs his way of thinking and acting. The ordinary life, the life which others still cling to in sadness, becomes "death" as Christ rightly called it when understood from the safety and peace of God's Presence. The human being, able to withdraw for an objective understanding of the world and other human beings, begins to understand how many times we substitute false or apparent goods for the actual truths. That soul, that human being, discovers several other things as well.

We talk on and on about many problems in life, and we gossip and we chat about nothing at all. The radios in our cars and the TVs in our homes fill our ears with terrible noises made in the name of love, or they spill over with the news about local and national disasters. We become inundated, filled to the brim with things that are not even of our nature. The world in which we live so crams us with nonsense that we tire of everything and develop a deaf ear, a kind of apathy that is, in truth, a paralysis.

Gift of Silence

The soul that is recollected—the soul that learns to shut off thoughts about people and worries about things that are only material—soon discovers that silence is a strange and wondrous commodity. That person begins to understand the gift of silence for himself and his senses. Just as an ear can be deafened by too loud or too long a stimulation, so can a human being become warped by too many demands and too many distractions.

To a great extent, we have lost the art of conversation in this land, and we are fast losing the power of thinking as well. The mass media, though wonderful in many respects, poses a grave danger of reducing men to passive recipients of an endless stream of images and sensations. People who listen to music or watch television all day will find it very difficult to think for themselves.

Hitler's propaganda ministers realized the power of the media and skillfully used and abused it for their own ends. By constantly inundating the people with hypnotic martial chants, empty slogans, and outright lies they reduced the people to a thoughtless submissive mass.

Silence restores us to ourselves by giving our brains a chance to function without the distraction and the chaos of noise or idiocy. Silence also gives us a chance to stand aside, slightly out of step with the parade, to look at the parade for what it is and to determine our own potential and our own unique destiny. The ancient Chinese cautioned their believers to live in a quiet house at the side of the road where they could ponder life without being involved.

We have our own model, Christ, who always returned to the service of others after a sojourn in the desert or time spent alone in the wilderness. So it is with us. We need time to be alone so that we can discover why we serve, why we compete, why we love others. For us it must not be a vain pursuit or something done merely in reaction. The Christian must do more than react; he must act, and not only follow but lead in the way of love.

If we practice the Presence of God, having withdrawn to a certain distance from our fellow human beings, even from all that is vain and petty in our own natures, we will discover two things: freedom and genuine charity of love.

Freedom and True Charity

Once we stand aside from the mad rush of the world to look back at it, we will discover in retrospect and meditation that we do not really need the world at all. We do not even need the people in it. This will startle us and perhaps make us feel guilty. To realize that God is enough and that all the relatives and friends, no matter how wonderful they may be, cannot fulfill us, will stun our senses, will tax our brains. The pain and the longings and the fitful desires that we knew will begin to slip off, and we will be free. We will begin to understand God's knowledge of the world. As St. Thomas Aquinas says:

> There is a special comfort in appreciating God's knowledge of us and of our world. It is a dreadful thing to be totally unknown. The bleakest reaches of loneliness do not quite touch such fearful isolation; for, however lonely we are, we are among our fellows who at least know what we are, for all their disregard of who we are or where our dreams are calling us. Even when loneliness is routed by the eager companionship of love, we writhe in an agony beyond human relief, of not being known enough and not knowing enough; in this sense we are always alone, alone because we cannot say all that is within us, cannot see all that is in the one we love. The fear of discovery that haunts our secret hours is a terror of inimical or indifferent hearts; it is only to our enemies that we fear to be known. Where love and understanding are guaranteed, it is not pain but blessed relief to have even our

most despicable weakness seen and administered to. That 'all things are naked and open to His eyes' (Heb. 4:13) is not to our terror but to the banishment of our deepest loneliness; it is to our constant comfort to remember that He reaches 'even to the division of the soul and the spirit, of the joints also and the marrow, and is a discerner of the thoughts and the intents of the heart; neither is there any creature invisible in His sight' (Heb. 4: 12-13). (St. Thomas, *My Way of Life*, Pt. 1, 11, 2)

The Practice of the Presence of God will lead you to understand God's knowledge of the world, and at the same time it will give you your freedom, out of yourself and your own needs. You will quite suddenly realize the intrinsic value of every human being that you meet. You will discover that God created this human being for Himself. How can you use or abuse a creature of God? How can you expect that creature to serve you alone or to defend you or to cater to your whims? How can you abase and humiliate, wound or scar such a being?

Understanding God's love for that human being, for all human beings, will place them in a distinct category, one that will make you hesitate and ponder. You will learn to love all men not for what they can do for you, but for themselves. If they wound you, you will worry more about the injury being done to them, by their actions, than your own pain. You will defend others and assist them without expecting a return, because you will understand that you serve God in this manner. Christ asked this of us.

Christ in Others

Begin to see Christ in everyone you meet. This does not mean that you have to live with the mad delusion that all men are Christlike. This means that what you endure for them, what you give them in service, in gentle kindness, in consideration is actually what you are rendering to Christ. If you are abused in return or considered a lunatic or stupid, do not let that worry you. God knows. You do not serve others for themselves, unless you know very little about people or the world. You, a Christian, serve Christ in the persons of those you meet. Then you will be as the one who comes upon the scene to radiate the joy of Christ, the grace of tireless devotion. Others will be startled by what they see and will follow Christ themselves.

Christ The Center of Our Life—Being Oneself

This Practice of the Presence of God, this living with Christ as the center of our being, means more than just conforming to His Will. It means turning ourselves inside out to reflect His beauty, His truth, His goodness, His mercy. The Apostolate of Christian Renewal means just this. Still, people have the mistaken idea that we all have to end up as replicas of one dead martyr. The world no longer has room for carbon copies of pious maidens or gallant knights. This world needs honest people who understand themselves. Let the seal of Christ be on you, as you are. Accept the problems of your personality and ask Christ to assist you with grace enough to overcome them. Understand your virtues as well and work to make them stronger. Don't try to become a plaster statue that looks lovely in the niche over the high altar.

In nature plants and animals reach perfection by fulfilling their essence. This means that a tree is a perfect tree if it functions entirely the way it should and fulfills the purpose for its existence. A tree that becomes something else in part would not be a perfect tree because it would be mutilated, outside the form which God intended for it. So it is with man. You are unique. Christ died for you, the way you are, knowing your wretched sins and your weaknesses. He died to give you the chance to change in Him, through the influence of the Holy Spirit. This means to perfect yourself as the unique person you are. This means to take on yourself the more perfect way of living, with your talents and intellect, your home life and your prayer life as well.

If you do not give praise to God, no one exactly like you will do it, for there is no one exactly like you. If you do not help a friend, neighbor, or stranger, no one will help that person in the special way that you could do it. God gave you specific tasks to perform, as Cardinal Newman's meditation states. You must perform these tasks, or they will not be accomplished.

The Practice of the Presence of God is the first step toward union with our Lord and the living of the Apostolate of Christian Renewal. It is a giant step, and it is one that you will have to take again and again. Day by day, as you slowly turn yourself toward giving praise instead of fretting, serving instead of asking to be served, keeping silent instead of raving about yourself, you will see the practice becoming easier, as God gives Himself more fully to you.

Slowly you will come to realize that it is not difficult to be alone or forgotten. You will cherish this because it will be one more time in which Christ can repay you Himself. You will come to realize that people around you are not as selfish or ugly as you believed. They just do not take you as seriously as you take yourself. Each man has his own problems, his own pains, his own dreams of eternity. When you no longer claim each man for your own, you will see that he comes to you willingly. You will be giving love as your gift to your fellowman.

Love is a transcendental. It cannot be held or smothered or chained. In other words, to renew itself, it must be given away. See the saints, who knew they were not worth much in the sight of God as far as merit is concerned, and you will see people that were loved by men.

Renewal—A Conversion

As we stated before, in the Apostolate of Christian Renewal you are asked to transform your life, exactly as it is, into a *metanoia*, a total conversion. This is important. You must realize that your own present state of life is the one in which you must perfect yourself. If you spend hours in prayer and let your children suffer you are deluding yourself. Learn to translate the housework, the lawn care, the chauffering of the family, your work into acts of service and praise for God. Snatch moments in the midst of these to offer praise until your entire life becomes one long hymn of praise.

If you join every known Catholic organization to prove you are reformed and leave your family home nights and weekends, then you are also wrong. Respect the life to which God has called you and perform your services through that life.

The Practice of the Presence of God can change the drab chores of life into contentment and peace. It can change the limitations of jobs, homes, neighborhoods, or families into spinning circles of warmth and love and praise. The challenge is yours. The challenge lies in the fact that you can turn yourselves away from the topsy-turvy values of the world into the realization of God's knowledge of the world and of His love for man.

Joy of a Christian

Those who come to Christ, through Mary, in the Spirit, develop particular signs in themselves that give comfort to others, and the greatest of these signs is joy. The letters and writings of all the saints and mystics show a distinct overflowing of happiness. This should be your mark as well in your life as a Christian.

Anyone who understands the news he hears on television, who really understands the headlines in the papers, finds very little to rejoice over today. When we see some with pie-in-the-sky ideas for making the world over, we shake our heads and go on our way, knowing that this person is not a realist. Still we are asked to have joy as Christians.

Pope Paul VI explains how this is not only possible but actually necessary in our time.

> But the Christian is a man of hope, and does not know despair. There is a difference between the Christian and the secular man in regard to hope. The latter is a *Vir desideriorum*, a man of many desires ... the man of desires seeks to shorten the distance between himself and the goods to be attained; he is a man of short-term hopes; he wants to satisfy them soon. Tangible, economic and temporal hopes are more easily satisfied; they are therefore quickly exhausted, become empty, and often leave the heart disappointed. His hopes do not ennoble the mind; they do not give life its full meaning and they turn the course of life among paths of questionable progress.
>
> But the Christian is the man of true hope, that which aims at attaining the supreme good (cf. St. Augustine's *Fecisti nos ad te* (Conf. 1:1). He knows that in his efforts to attain his desire he has the help of that supreme Good which unites with hope the confidence and the

grace to fulfill it. (Pope Paul VI, *Christian Hope Is the Answer to World Problems*, 6)

As we become mature Christians, we look at life in a different manner, in the Presence of God. We discover the place of grace within us as individual human beings and within the whole of mankind, in God's plan of salvation. This raises our hearts, our minds, our souls to a level beyond that of the ordinary person on earth.

> Truly the story of grace is a story of Divine Love. Its magnificence holds us breathless. Through grace we are no longer slaves to sin or imprisoned in this world. We are the sons of God. And if we are His sons, then we are His heirs too. Ultimate happiness is within our grasp. The Love of God for us offers to us the gift of ecstatic happiness. We have but to reach out for it and grasp it in love. The Love of God calls to us for our love. The reward is God Himself. Who would refuse? (St. Thomas Aquinas, *Summa Theologica*, XIV, 10)

Desire To Share

We will be so filled with the Presence of God, so imbued with His grace and His Divine Will, that our hearts will glow with enthusiasm to spread the Gospel, the Good News. Dryness, apathy, misunderstanding, abuse, will not shrivel our hearts because we will understand the limits of time and press on toward the Ultimate Happiness which Christ bought for us with the Cross.

The Cross—Stamp or Seal of a Christian

The Cross, that wretched sign of pain and cruelty, will become a thing of joy for us. We will look upon Christ in His agony, and we will understand, at least, the gifts of life He gave us in dying. And we will remember the words of St. John:

> No one can show greater love than this: to lay down his life for those he loves (Jn. 15:13). I am the good shepherd; the good shepherd lays down his life for the sheep ... I am the good shepherd: I know my sheep and mine know me ... And for these sheep I lay down my life. (John 10: 11-15)

Also the words of St. Paul, 'For God has made Him Who knew no sin to be sin for us, that we might be made the justice of God in Him. (2 Cor. 5:21)

Christ died upon the Cross, the symbol of condemnation and loathing. His Body was pinned to a tree and raised above the earth that all might see Him and mock Him and despise Him. They laughed and lunged at His robes and pierced His side. And then they did not laugh. The centurion on guard at the foot of the Cross proclaimed for all to hear that this was the Son of God. And the world discovered that the Cross, the sign of the wretched and the criminal, was the sign of life for us all. With the saints we can call the fall a happy fault because our very weakness, and our pitiful wretchedness, brought us such a redeemer.

Constantine, on the battlefield, saw the Cross in the heavens and heard a voice saying: "In this sign shall you conquer." We are modern Constantines. We stand on our own battlefields as a nation, as neighbors, as individuals. We know the enemies that surround us, as we know the enemy within us all. This shall be our sign also. The Cross of Christ is our hope, and our Joy.

If we are asked to carry our own crosses, how can we despair? We can carry the crosses Christ sends to us. He understands us well and gives us His help to bear them—crosses that will root out the death within us and bring us to perfection in Him. We can also help carry the crosses of others. This is the ultimate act of service, and we are capable of it. Rejoice in the Cross. Rejoice in the love of Christ on the Cross. Bear the Cross proudly and happily when it comes to you, and radiate your own sure knowledge of His love for you. This is Christian joy. This is living in God's Presence and understanding the world as He knows it. This is the Christian Renewal we seek for ourselves and our families.

PRAYER IN CHRISTIAN RENEWAL

To reach the exalted state of being constantly aware of the Presence of God, we need to be men of prayer. Unfortunately, we live in a time when many do not pray or even think that it is not necessary to pray. We hear it said that we should pray only when we feel like it, or when it fulfills us, or when it is meaningful to us. Our model should be Christ. And how did He regard prayer in His life? All we need to do is to open the Good Book, the Bible, and we can see for ourselves.

Prayer In Christ's Life

Prayer held a very great, important place in Our Lord's life. Even the feverish activity of His apostolic life did not prevent Him from spending time in private prayer. We see Him spending long hours in total recollection throughout the night, or in the early hours of dawn. We see Him go into the hills, into the desert, or spend time at the seashore in prayer. He prays especially in times of temptation, or in moments of fear. (Mk. 14, 32ff; Lk. 9: 10; Lk. 21:37; Mt. 14:23; Mt. 26:36; Lk. 3, 21; Lk. 21:34-37)

Before great decisions or important moments in His life Christ prays: before He chooses the Apostles (Lk. 6:12-16), before Peter's profession of faith (Lk. 9:18), before the Transfiguration (Lk. 9:20), before teaching us the Our Father (Lk. 11:1). During His activities, He praises His Father for always listening to Him (Jn. 11:41). At the end of a hard day in apostolic work, He gives thanks to God (Mk. 1:35); and after the power or goodness of God is shown, He thanks His Heavenly Father (Mk. 6: 46).

Sharing in Community Praying

Christ was faithful to community praying as well. We see Him partaking and sharing in the official liturgy of the synagogue on the Sabbath and the annual Passover (Mt. 13:54; 26:54, 4:23; 21:12; 24:1, 26: 1-5).

Thus we have the example of Christ, and we, too, should esteem prayer as a necessary part of our lives. We should pray in private as well as in community.

The disciples asked our Lord to teach them how to pray and He answered: "Pray then like this: 'Our Father, who are in heaven —" (Mt. 6:9). If we analyze this prayer we see that it is a perfect prayer of adoration and petition. He asked us to pray in His name and assured us that everything we asked in His Name we would receive from the Father.

> Whatever you ask in My Name, I will do it, that the Father may be glorified in the Son. (Jn 14:13)
>
> If you ask anything of the Father, he will give it to you in my name. (Jn 16:23)

Finally, He tells us that the Holy Spirit can be obtained through prayer: "If you then, who are evil, know how to give good gifts to your children, how much more will the heavenly Father give the Holy Spirit to those who ask Him." (Lk. 11:13)

Attitude in Praying

Christ also teaches us in what spirit and with what attitude we should pray; with the insistence of the widow before the unjust judge (Lk. 18:1-8; Mt. 7:7-11); with the secrecy of him who acts not to be seen by men (Mt. 6: 5-6); with the sincerity of him who speaks not from the lips alone (Mt. 6:7-8; 7:21); with the humility of him who does not think himself superior to anyone (Lk 18: 9-14 Mt. 7:15); with the simplicity of a heart without bitterness (Mt. 6:14; 18: 23-25); with total confidence in the Providence of the Father: "Whatever you ask in prayer, you will receive, if you have faith." (Mt. 21:22; 6:25-34; 7: 7-11) (cf. Congregation of the Sacred Hearts, Rule of Life, 55)

Prayer requires effort and a personal commitment with a conscientious response to the Word of God. You will have to constantly purify and renew yourself if you wish to maintain a sense of values in our modern world, and if you wish to have a strong and living faith. It is a time of continuing renewal in a joyous submission to faith.

Holy Scripture

Our prayer must be nourished and built on the Word of God.

If not, it will be fragile and questionable because it will be built on a morality, on a tradition, or on rites.

> For the word of God is living and active, sharper than any two-edged sword, piercing to the division of soul and spirit of joints and marrow, and discerning the thoughts and intentions of the heart. And before him no creature is hidden, but all are open and laid to the eyes of him with whom we have to do. (Heb. 4: 12-13)

It is only in the Scriptures as interpreted by the living tradition of the Church that we will find the convictions of faith which must support our actions with men.

> —This sacred Synod earnestly and specifically urges all the Christian faithful, too, especially religious, to learn by frequent reading of the Divine Scriptures the 'excelling knowledge of Jesus Christ' (St. Jerome, *Commentary on Isaiah* Prol.; PL 24:17). Therefore, they should gladly put themselves in touch with the sacred text itself, whether it be through the Liturgy, rich in the Divine Word, or through devotional reading, or through instructions suitable for the purpose and other aids which, in our time, are commendably available everywhere, thanks to the approval and active support of the shepherds of the Church. And let them remember that prayer should accompany the reading of Sacred Scripture, so that God and man may talk together; for 'We speak to Him when we pray; we hear Him when we read the Divine sayings' (St. Ambrose, *On the Duties of Ministers*, 1, 20, 88; PL 16:50) (Vat. II, *Revelation*, 25)

When we read Holy Scripture, we should remember that it is the Word of God speaking to us (1 Thess. 2:13), and when we hear the Word of God we should not be hearers only, but actively put it into practice. (Lk. 6, 46-49; Jas. 1: 19-25) Let it be the light that illuminates your life (2 Peter 1, 19).

Liturgy: Sacrifice, Sacraments, Banquet

The Holy Spirit gives us a deep appreciation and love for the Liturgy, that is the holy sacrificial banquet and the Sacraments. We are given the privilege of participating in the priesthood of Christ and it is through the Liturgy that we are able to exercise our priesthood.

> Christ the Lord, High Priest taken from among men (cf. Heb. 5: 1-5) made a kingdom and priests to God His Father (Apoc. 1:6; cf. 5:9-10) out of this new people. The baptized by regeneration and the anointing of the Holy Spirit, are consecrated into a spiritual house and a holy priesthood. Thus through all those works befitting Christian men they can offer spiritual sacrifices and proclaim the power of Him who has called them out of darkness into His marvelous light (cf. 1 Peter 2: 4:10). Therefore all the disciples of Christ, persevering in prayer and praising God (cf. Acts 2: 42-47), should present themselves as a living sacrifice, holy and pleasing to God (cf. Rom. 12:1). Everywhere on earth they must bear witness to Christ and give an answer to those who seek an account of that hope of eternal life which is in them. (cf. 1 Pet. 3:15)
>
> Though they differ from one another in essence and not only in degree, the common priesthood of the faithful and the ministerial or hierarchical priesthood are nonetheless interrelated. Each of them in its own special way is a participation in the one priesthood of Christ. The ministerial priest, by the sacred power he enjoys, molds and rules the priestly people. Acting in the person of Christ, he brings about the Eucharistic Sacrifice, and offers it to God in the name of all the people. For their part, the faithful join in the offering of the Eucharist by virtue of their royal priesthood. They likewise exercise that priesthood by receiving the sacraments, by prayer and thanksgiving, by the witness of a holy life, and by self-denial and active charity. (Vat. II, *The Church,* 10)

We can see the importance of the Sacraments and the practice of virtue in our spiritual life because the priestly community operates through them.

> It is through the Sacraments and the exercise of the virtues that the sacred nature and organic structure of the priestly community is brought into operation. Incorporated into the Church through baptism, the faithful are consecrated by the baptismal character to the exercise of the cult of the Christian religion. Reborn as sons of God, they must confess before men the faith they have received from God through the Church. Bound more intimately to the Church by the Sacrament of Confirmation, they are endowed by the Holy Spirit with special strength. Hence they are more strictly obliged to spread and defend the faith both by word and deed as true witnesses of Christ.

On the night Christ was betrayed, He instituted the Sacrament of His Body and Blood to perpetuate the sacrifice of the Cross throughout the centuries, until His coming.

At the Last Supper, on the night when He was betrayed, Our Savior instituted the Eucharistic Sacrifice of His Body and Blood. He did this in order to perpetuate the sacrifice of the Cross throughout the centuries until He should come again, and to entrust to His beloved spouse, the Church, a memorial of His death and resurrection: A sacrament of love, a sign of unity, a bond of charity, a paschal banquet in which Christ is consumed, the mind is filled with grace and a pledge of future glory is given to us. (Vat. II, *Liturgy*, 47)

In this way, honor and glory are given to God the Father through the sacrifice offered by the priest from the rising of the sun to the setting thereof.

—The Priest alone can complete the building up of the Body in the Eucharistic Sacrifice. Thus are fulfilled the Words of God spoken through His prophet: 'From the rising of the sun even to the going down My Name is great among the Gentiles, and in every place there is sacrifice, and there is offered to My Name a clean oblation' (Mal. 1:11). In this way the Church simultaneously prays and labors in order that the entire world may become the People of God, the Body of the Lord, and the Temple of the Holy Spirit, and that in Christ, the Head of all, there may be rendered to the Creator, and Father of the Universe all honor and glory. (Vat. II, *The Church*, 17)

The Common Priesthood

The People of God exercise their priesthood whenever they participate in the offering of the Eucharistic sacrifices, in which they are able to unite themselves, their lives, their own work and all creation with the Divine Victim.

Taking part in the Eucharistic Sacrifice, which is the fount and apex of the whole Christian life, they offer the Divine Victim to God, and offer themselves along with it. Thus both by the act of oblation and through Holy Communion, all perform their proper part in this liturgical service, not, indeed, all in the same way but each in that way which is appropriate to himself. (Vat. II, *The Church*, 11)

Through the exercise of their priestly function, the laity can consecrate the world itself to God.

For besides intimately associating them with His life and His mission,

Christ also gives them a share in His priestly function of offering spiritual worship for the glory of God and the salvation of men. For this reason the laity, dedicated to Christ and anointed by the Holy Spirit, are marvelously called and equipped to produce in themselves ever more abundant fruit of the Holy Spirit. For all their works, prayers, and apostolic endeavors, their ordinary married and family life, their daily duties, their mental and physical relaxation, if carried out in the Spirit, and even the hardships of life, if patiently born—all of these become spiritual sacrifices acceptable to God through Jesus Christ (cf. 1 Peter 2:5). During the celebration of the Eucharist, these sacrifices are most lovingly offered to the Father along with the Lord's body. Thus, as worshipers whose every deed is holy, the laity consecrate the world itself to God. (Vat. II, *The Church*, 34)

For this reason the People of God come together and assemble and offer worship to God. The Eucharistic celebration is the highest expression of community prayer. Therefore we should not only feel obliged to participate in the Eucharistic celebrations, but we should consider it a great privilege and honor. If we but understood what is happening at Mass, what we are doing there, we would participate more joyfully in the Eucharistic celebration.

—For, through the apostolic proclamation of the gospel, the People of God is called together and assembled so that when all who belong to this People have been sanctified by the Holy Spirit, they can offer themselves as 'a sacrifice, living, holy, pleasing to God' (Rom. 12:1). Through the ministry of priests, the spiritual sacrifice of the faithful is made perfect in union with the sacrifice of Christ, the sole Mediator. Through the hands of priests and in the name of the whole Church, the Lord's sacrifice is offered in the Eucharist in an unbloody and sacramental manner until He Himself returns. (Vat. II, *Priests*, 2)

The Eucharistic Sacrifice

When we are offering the Eucharistic sacrifice, we are not acting alone as an individual, but together as the People of God, as a family. We are offering the hopes and desires, the joys and sorrows, the prayers and sacrifices, the labors and sufferings, the acts of love and adoration, the acts of thanksgiving and reparation, acts of petitions for ourselves and for others. All these become united into the one great prayer—the Eucharistic prayer. In the Eucharistic sacrifice our prayers become Christ's prayer and

His prayer becomes our prayer. Christian communion among the faithful brings us closer to Christ.

The Saints And The Liturgy

We are also united with the saints in heaven and they contribute greatly to the up-building of the Church. We can invite them to pray for us, with us, and through us.

> But in various ways and degrees we all partake in the same love of God and neighbor, and all sing the same hymn of glory to our God. For all who belong to Christ, having His Spirit, form one Church and cleave together in Him (cf. Eph. 4:16). Therefore the union of the wayfarers with the brethren who have gone to sleep in the peace of Christ is not in the least interrupted. On the contrary, according to the perennial faith of the Church, it is strengthened through the exchanging of spiritual goods.
> For by reason of the fact that those in heaven are more closely united with Christ, they establish the whole Church more firmly in holiness, lend nobility to the worship which the Church offers on earth to God, and in many ways contribute to its greater upbuilding (cf. 1 Cor. 12:12-27). For after they have been received into their heavenly home and are present to the Lord (cf. 2 Cor. 5:8), through Him and with Him and in Him, they do not cease to intercede with the Father for us. Rather, they show forth the merits which they won on earth through the one Mediator between God and men, Christ Jesus (cf. 1 Tim. 2:5). There they served God in all things and filled up in their flesh whatever was lacking of the sufferings of Christ on behalf of His body which is the Church (cf. Col. 1:24). Thus by their brotherly interest our weakness is very greatly strengthened. (Vat. II, *The Church*, 49)

Our communion with the saints in heaven and the souls in purgatory brings us closer to Christ and unites us all in a common bond of unity and love.

> This most sacred Synod accepts with great devotion the venerable faith of our ancestors regarding this vital fellowship with our brethren who are in heavenly glory or who are still being purified after death. (Vat. II, *The Church*, 51)
> For just as Christian communion among the wayfarers brings us closer to Christ, so our companionship with the saints joins us to Christ

from Whom as from their fountain and head issue every grace and the life of God's people itself. (Vat. II, *The Church,* 50)

And Christ brings us to God, His heavenly Father and our Father.

It is supremely fitting, therefore, that we love those friends and fellow heirs of Jesus Christ, who are also our brothers and extraordinary benefactors, that we render due thanks to God for them and 'Suppliantly invoke them and have recourse to their prayers, their power and help in obtaining benefits from God through His Son, Jesus Christ, Our Lord, who is our sole Redeemer and Savior.' For by its very nature every genuine testimony of love which we show to those in heaven tends toward and terminates in Christ who is the 'Crown of all saints.' Through Him it tends toward and terminates in God, who is wonderful in His saints and is magnified in them. (Vat. II, *The Church,* 50)

Our union with the Saints in heaven is brought about more effectively when we offer the Eucharistic sacrifice together.

Our union with the Church in heaven is put into effect in its noblest manner when with common rejoicing we celebrate together the praise of the Divine Majesty. Then all those from every tribe and tongue and people and nation (cf. Apoc. 5:9) who have been redeemed by the blood of Christ and gathered together into one Church, with one song of praise magnify the one and Triune God. Such is especially the case of the Sacred Liturgy, where the power of the Holy Spirit acts upon us through sacramental signs. Celebrating the Eucharistic sacrifice, therefore, we are most closely united in the worshipping Church in heaven as we join with and venerate the memory first of all of the glorious ever-virgin Mary, of Blessed Joseph and the blessed apostles and martyrs, and all the saints. (Vat. II, *The Church,* 50)

Our fellowship with the heavenly court enhances the worship that we offer to God the Father, through Christ, in the Spirit.

...At the same time, let the people be instructed that our communion with those in heaven, provided that it is understood in the more adequate light of faith, in no way weakens, but conversely, more thoroughly enriches the supreme worship we give God the Father, through Christ, in the Spirit. (Vat. II, *The Church,* 51)

Liturgical Reform

The Eucharistic sacrificial banquet has been reformed so that the People of God may more actively participate in the Divine Worship, that they may more clearly exercise their priesthood. The structure of the Mass has been changed so that we now have the Liturgy of the Word and the Liturgy of the Eucharist. They are so closely linked with one another that they form one single act of worship.

> The two parts which, in a certain sense, go to make up the Mass, namely, the liturgy of the word and the Eucharistic Liturgy are so closely connected with each other that they form but one single worship. Accordingly this sacred Synod strongly urges pastors of souls that, when instructing the faithful, they insistently teach them to take their part in the entire Mass, especially on Sundays and feasts of obligation. (Vat. II, *The Liturgy*, 56)

Liturgy of The Word

The liturgy of the word consists of the entrance song or prayer, the expression of our sinfulness and asking for forgiveness, praising God in the Gloria, the Scriptural readings in the collect, epistles and gospel, the homily, creed and prayer of the faithful. The liturgy of the word is filled with Scriptural sayings, and thus God speaks to us through the treasures contained in the Holy Bible.

> The treasures of the Bible are to be opened up more lavishly, so that richer fare may be provided for the faithful at the table of God's Word. In this way a more representative portion of the Holy Scriptures will be read to the people over a set cycle of years. (Vat. II, *The Liturgy*, 51)

The homily is an important part of the liturgy of the word because it is to explain the Scriptural sayings, and make them relevant to present world situations and problems of life.

> By means of the homily the mysteries of the faith and the guiding principles of the Christian life are expounded from the sacred text

during the course of the liturgical year. The homily, therefore, is to be highly esteemed as part of the Liturgy itself; in fact, at those Masses which are celebrated with the assistance of the people on Sundays and the feasts of obligation, it should not be omitted except for a serious reason. (Vat. II, *The Liturgy,* 52)

It is the duty of the priest to proclaim that Gospel of the Lord so that faith may be instilled deeper into the hearts of the People of God.

> The People of God finds its unity first of all through the Word of the living God, which is quite properly sought from the lips of priests. Since no one can be saved who has not first believed, priests, as co-workers with their bishops, have as their primary duty the proclamation of the Gospel of God to all. In this way they fulfill the Lord's command: 'Go into the whole world and preach the gospel to every creature' (Mk. 16:15). Thus they establish and build up the People of God.
>
> For through the saving Word the spark of faith is struck in the hearts of unbelievers, and fed in the hearts of the faithful. By this faith the community of the faithful begins and grows. As the Apostle says: Faith depends on hearing and hearing on the word of Christ (Rom. 10: 17). (Vat. II, *Priests,* 4)

Priestly preaching must apply Christ's teachings to concrete circumstances so that the faithful may receive more benefit from these eternal truths.

> No doubt, priestly preaching is often very difficult in the circumstances of the modern world. If it is to influence the mind of the listener more fruitfully, such preaching must not present God's Word in a general and abstract fashion only, but it must apply the perennial truth of the gospel to the concrete circumstances of life. (Vat. II, *Priests,* 4)

The priest should not be afraid to teach the truths of Christ, even when inconvenient.

> ... They should act toward men, not as seeking to win their favor but in accord with the demands of Christian doctrine and life. They should teach and admonish men as dearly beloved sons, according to the words of the Apostle: 'Be urgent in season, out of season; reprove, entreat, rebuke with all patience and teaching' (2 Tim. 4:2). (Vat. II, *Priests,* 6)

After the homily, we profess what we believe in the creed. The creed is a summation of the principal articles of faith which all true Catholics profess. Following the creed, we have the prayer of the faithful; petitioning God to be favorable to our needs.

> Especially on Sundays and feasts of obligation, there is to be restored, after the gospel and homily, 'the common prayer' or 'the prayer of the faithful.' By this prayer, in which the people are to take part, intercession will be made for Holy Church, for the civil authorities, for those oppressed by various needs, for all mankind, and for the salvation of the entire world. (cf. 1 Tim. 2: 1-2) (Vat. II, *Liturgy*, 53)

Liturgy of The Eucharist

After the prayer of the faithful the Liturgy of the Eucharist begins. The gifts are brought to the altar by representatives of the faithful. The Liturgy of the Eucharist consists of the offertory, the canon—in which the sacrifice is made and the Sacrament of the Eucharist is confected; Holy Communion, the banquet of the Lord, and the period of thanksgiving.

At the offertory, we offer the gifts and ourselves to God.

> ...At the table of the Lord's Body, they should give thanks to God, by offering the Immaculate Victim, not only through the hands of the priest, but also with him, they should learn to offer themselves too. Through Christ the Mediator, they should be drawn day by day into ever closer union with God and with each other, so that finally God may be all in all. (Vat. II, *Liturgy*, 48)

The canon of the Mass is the apex of the Eucharistic service because at the Consecration, the Sacrifice of the Lord is made to His Heavenly Father, and Christ becomes present, Body, Blood, Soul and Divinity. He is present sacramentally in His resurrected state. We, together with Christ, are offered to the Father; Christ's sacrifice becomes our sacrifice, and our prayers become His prayer.

The banquet of the Lord, or the meal as it is often called, begins with the Our Father. We have the privilege of partaking the Body of the Lord as our spiritual food.

For the Most Blessed Eucharist contains the Church's entire spiritual wealth, that is, Christ Himself, our Passover and living bread. Through His very flesh, made vital and vitalizing by the Holy Spirit, He offers life to men. (Vat. II, *Priests*, 5)

This, then is our Mass, ever old and ever new. We honor and worship God in the manner Christ said we should. We also celebrate a victory over death and sin, which was won by Christ. We take part in Christ's passion, death, resurrection, and ascension. We have reason to rejoice and be filled with happiness since His victory is our victory. Every Mass is Easter Sunday.

Liturgy, Sign of Covenant

The Mass is also a sign of the covenant made between God and us. In the Old Testament it is related how God chose Abraham and made a covenant with him. He said that the Isrealites would be His people if they remained faithful to Him, and that He would be their God. He promised to remain faithful to them. This covenant was sealed by the blood of the circumcision and the blood sacrifices of animals. Christ came to make a new covenant with the People of God and it is sealed with His own Blood on the cross and renewed in each Mass. We are His People, He is our God.

Presence of Christ

Therefore, the Mass should be the center of our day; it should be the highlight of our life. Everything should revolve around this tremendous act of sacrificial worship. We should be eucharistic souls, burning with love and zeal for Christ, who is present in the Blessed Sacrament in the Tabernacle as well. Christ in the Blessed Sacrament remains at the center of the Family of God.

We all know that Christ is present when two or more are gathered in His Name, present when the Scriptures are read in Church, present in the person of the ministers, present in each Sacrament in which each has a particular role to play in our lives. But it is especially in the Eucharist that the Presence of God is given us in its fullness.

The Presence of Christ in the Blessed Sacrament is a constant reminder of the permanent Presence of Christ in His Church to maintain it in unity. It is a sign of God's fidelity to the new covenant He made with us, and it is an invitation for us to be faithful to Him.

When we are praying before the Blessed Sacrament we are face to face with the Supreme Reality. We become aware that we have our Lord, the glorious Lamb with the marks of His sacrifice, offering Himself to His Father on our behalf. He offers the thankful adoration of all redeemed creation, the prayers of reparation for sinners, and for the needs of mankind.

An apostle of Christian Renewal should spend some time, if even only five minutes, before the Blessed Sacrament. This should be a daily practice whenever possible.

Sacrament of Reconciliation

The Sacrament of Reconciliation, or penance, is meant to be a Sacrament of love, of peace, and of mercy. Christ instituted this Sacrament after His resurrection from the dead.

> ...And when He had said this, He breathed on them, and said to them, Receive the Holy Spirit. If you forgive the sins of any, they are forgiven; if you retain the sins of any, they are retained. (Jn. 20: 22-23)

Those who take part in the Sacrament of Penance have their sins forgiven through the power and mercy of Christ. They are reconciled with God, whom they have offended by their sins, and also with the Church, which they have wounded by their sins.

It is important to try to go to the same confessor so that he may get to know you. He also should be the guardian and guide in your spiritual life. Just as a plant needs a gardener to help it mature to fruitfulness, so each soul needs a spiritual director to guide it to spiritual maturity.

Sacrament of the Sick

Through the Sacrament of the Sick, the anointing of the sick and the prayers of priests, the whole Church commends those who are ill to the suffering and glorified Lord. He is asked to lighten their sufferings and to save them. The Church also exhorts them to associate themselves with the passion and death of our Lord so that they may contribute to the welfare of the whole People of God.

Holy Orders

Those who are consecrated to the service of God through Holy Orders, are appointed to feed the Church in Christ's name with the word and grace of God.

Christian Marriage

Christian spouses, in virtue of the Sacrament of Matrimony, partake of the mystery of unity, and fruitful spiritual love, which exists between Christ and His Church. The married partners are to help each other to attain holiness in their married life. Together they are to rear and educate their offspring, for from the wedlock of Christians come Christian families, who will perpetuate the People of God through the centuries. The family is meant to be a domestic Church. It is the parents who become the first teachers and preachers of faith to their children. This they do by their words and example.

Liturgy, Summit of Church's Activity

The Sacred Liturgy does not exhaust the entire activity of the Church because, before coming to the liturgy, people must be called to faith and conversion. Nevertheless the liturgy is the summit toward which all activity of the Church is directed; it is at the same time the foundation, source, or fountain from which all Her powers flow. The goal of all apostolic works is that all who are sons of God through baptism and faith should come together as a community to praise God in worship in Her sacrifice and to partake of the Lord's Supper.

The liturgy inspires the faithful to become one in heart and mind. The Eucharist draws men into a compelling love of Christ and sets them afire for the things of God. Therefore, from the

Eucharist grace is channeled into us for our sanctification and the glorification of God.

We must come to the liturgy with proper dispositions so that it may produce its full effect. We must realize what we are doing, matching our thoughts with our words and our actions in accordance with both. We should not go to liturgical services just to fulfill a rite or an obligation.

The spiritual life is not confined to participation in the liturgy. The Christian is called to pray together with his brethren, but also he is to pray alone in secret (cf. Mt. 6:6). As St. Paul tells us, we must learn to pray without ceasing (cf. 1 Th. 5:17). The same Apostle tells us that we must carry about in our body the dying of Jesus, that is dying to self, so that the life of Jesus may be made manifest in us, that is putting on Christ. (cf. 2 Cor. 4:10-11)

Put On Christ—Personal Commitment

Many people come to the realization that they are to put on Christ but they hesitate. Some feel that they are not worthy to make a personal commitment to Christ, or they fear that they will have to give up their desires, their pleasures. They are not strong enough in their convictions and they continue in life vacillating between the spirit of the world, the desires of the flesh, and the powerful attraction of God. People like this need encouragement to make their commitment, to become generous in accepting the Will of God for them.

We do not suggest that this commitment be made without due preparation because it is not meant to be emotional, sentimental, or superficial. It is meant to be a commitment for life. Therefore, at least a month's preparation is necessary so that we may have a solid foundation for living this commitment.

In order to live this commitment, we need to have a knowledge of the spirit of the world, ourselves, of the Blessed Ever Virgin Mary, and of Jesus Christ. Thus, the purpose of the Preparation.

After making the preparation, you are ready to make your commitment to Christ through Mary. This can be done either individually by yourself or in a group with a ceremony. I would advise the latter, but sometimes circumstances will not permit this to be done. It is well to renew our commitment every day so that we may be constantly aware of how we should be living our spiritual life.

True Zeal Not Sham

When we make this commitment to Jesus through Mary, usually we are filled with the love of God and with zeal for the things of God. This is wonderful, but it must be true and solid. It may not be a passing fancy, or it will wither and die; nor should it be misguided zeal, which would make pests of ourselves to others. It is true that we should encourage others to make a commitment to Christ through Mary, but this should be done by example and prayer. We should invite them to make a renewal of their spiritual life, but never by hounding them to the point that they think we are just fanatical fools. We must respect the rights of others, their freedom of conscience and their feelings. We may not act like a bull dog, forcing them to accept our way of thinking. All we have to do is to tell them about Christian renewal and leave them free to decide for themselves whether they wish to undertake this important step in spiritual living. We also must avoid giving the impression that we are better than anyone else, because in truth we are not. We are still sinful souls trying to achieve spiritual maturity.

Prayer Life And Renewal

Many people who have a metanoia, a change of heart, a conversion in their spiritual life, and make a commitment to Christ through Mary really begin to live their spiritual life as they should. They develop their prayer life in a proper way. But some get bogged down in things which are not really helpful in living the spiritual life. Their prayer life consists in reading many prayers, making novena after novena, and they join every organization they can find. If they are told not to follow this method of praying and acting they become indignant and tell you to mind your own business. Unfortunately, souls like this will never advance much in spiritual perfection. They actually think that they are praying and acting correctly, but in fact they are not.

Talking to God—Listening to God—Thinking of God

Formal prayer is good if it brings the soul to love God and neighbor more; if it leads to the practice of virtue and use of the gifts of the Holy Spirit which we received at baptism in an embryonic stage. But it is really meditative prayer that will bring these gifts and virtues to perfection. Meditation means that we learn to think about God, to talk with God in our own way. This method of praying comes easily to some, it did to the Little Flower. At an early age she would try to be alone to think about God, to offer her own prayers of adoration, thanksgiving, and petition to God. She also prayed for others, making reparation for their sins. She was actually meditating without knowing it.

Many people find it hard to meditate because they have never been taught how to talk with God or to think of God. In the beginning it would be helpful to use a book on spiritual matters or the Scriptures. Read the passage and think about it. Then, little by little, you will find that you are able to make acts of love, thanksgiving, sorrow for sin, and petition. As time passes, you become proficient in the art of meditating. Many times you will be filled with love and prayers will flow easily from the depth of your heart. You have a feeling of joy and happiness in praying and the time seems to pass much too quickly. You are able to think about God more and more through the day. God seems to be close and lavishing His consolation upon you. Gradually you no longer need the book to begin your meditation, but you are able to pray freely and almost without effort.

However, this will not last forever because as you advance in the spiritual life this form of meditation must give way to another one. Some people might never get beyond this form of praying, either because they are not generous enough, or God is bringing them to spiritual maturity at a slower pace.

Those souls who meditate in the manner just described will try hard to avoid serious sin in their lives, or if they have a habit of sinning seriously they will begin to overcome their weakness. We all know that we are sinners, and that we have to constantly strive against the spirit of the world, the devil, and the desires and passions within us. The more fully we are able to develop our spiritual life the less sin we will commit.

Types of Sinners

It is good at times to point out the various types of sinners. There are those who act through ignorance, like St. Paul before his conversion. He went about persecuting Christians until he had the vision of Christ. He tells us that God was merciful to him because he acted in ignorance, yet he did not excuse himself and say that he did not sin. When he learned that he was doing wrong he changed. Then we have those who sin through weakness, like St. Peter who because of fear denied Christ. Yet Our Lord had only to look at him and he wept bitter tears of repentance. He, too, recognized that he was a sinner. Finally, we have those who do things maliciously, like Judas. He, too, recognized that he was a sinner, but apparently did not ask for forgiveness. Our Lord said of him, "It would be better if that man had not been born;" yet we may not judge him—only God may do that.

We should also consider the various types of sin. Serious sin, which we call mortal sin, is a deliberate act or an omission of an act which would be death-bearing. A mortal sin separates us from the love of God and the love of our neighbor. If we commit this sin we turn our back upon God and freely separate ourselves from Him. It is saying no *to* God, and in effect telling Him that we do not want any part of Him. We are actually committing spiritual suicide because we destroy the life of God within us.

Venial sin is less serious and does not separate us from God; nevertheless it hinders us from advancing in the spiritual life. If we do not try to overcome venial faults we soon contract anemia of the soul, and we become weaker and more prone to fall into serious sin.

Finally, we have faults and failings which are classified as imperfections. These are acts or omissions which are done without thinking and thus they do not hinder us from advancing in the spiritual life. Yet, we should try to eliminate even imperfections from our lives. Of course, we will never succeed in completely eliminating them because we are human.

Acquired Contemplation

The person who meditates faithfully and conscientiously will come to a point in his spiritual development where he will find that he can no longer pray as before. The joy and happiness disappear and God seems to be far away from him. Prayer no longer flows easily and he experiences dryness and desolation. He may think that everything is lost and he misses the closeness and consolations of God. This is not a moment for despair, but one of consolation and hope.

It is necessary to have a good spiritual director at this point because he might have the temptation of giving up, saying, "What is the use of it?" It is good for the spiritual director to test the spirit to see whether God is actually calling him to a higher form of prayer. The director has to see whether he is really serious in living the spiritual life, or whether this is due to a lack of cooperation with God's graces and gifts.

When he finds that a person is genuinely serious in seeking God, through prayer and the practice of virtues, he must tell him to abandon the previous form of praying. Such a one should discontinue discursive meditation, which would only tax the intellect.

What has happened is that the will has taken over more and more in the spiritual life. Since the will is a blind faculty, much of the joy and happiness in praying disappears. Then the intellect, because it is less occupied, will wander more, and he will experience more distractions. Nevertheless, if his will is fixed on God, he will advance in the spiritual life.

Actually he already has advanced beyond the way of a beginner. He now finds it easier to perform acts of virtue and overcome venial sins. At this stage of development he will seldom fall into mortal sin. He may really suffer from the aridity he experiences because it is a purifying process of the senses, and this period of his development may last for years, or even his entire life time. On the other hand, God may bring him through this period quickly. The prayer in this stage of development is called acquired contemplation. Every soul has to go through this experience, more or less, to come to the next stage, or the mystical state.

One thing should be pointed out before speaking about prayer in the mystical state: when the soul has advanced to acquired contemplation it might not be able to exercise this type of prayer every day. The soul might, at times, have to go back to discursive mental prayer. Acquired contemplation means the ability to rest in the presence of God. The will is united with Him and prayer is going on without words.

To give you an example: Father Mateo, SS.CC. once met a man who could not read or write. Father talked to him about God and the man displayed a tremendous knowledge of the things of God. Father Mateo wanted him to write down his beautiful thoughts, but the man said, "I cannot read or write." Father Mateo asked him, "How did you come to such knowledge of God, and how do you pray?" The man answered, "When I sit before the tabernacle I look at God and He looks at me." God taught him through contemplative prayer.

It is important again for the spiritual director to pay close attention to what is going on in the soul during this period. He will have to test the spirit, and observe whether the soul is truly praying, or just wasting time. How will he know? Acquired contemplative prayer produces a deepening of the spiritual life. The virtues and gifts of the Holy Spirit begin to produce good wholesome effects in the soul. The soul not only keeps the Commandments but lives the Beatitudes described in the Sermon on the Mount. The soul is humble and obedient, but above all, charity is clearly seen to shine out for all to observe.

Infused Contemplation

As the person practices acquired contemplative prayer, he gradually comes closer to God and disposes himself for the mystical state. The mystical state begins with infused contemplative prayer. No one can obtain this exalted prayer by himself; rather it is a gift from God. A person can only dispose himself for it through prayer and the practice of virtue. The Holy Spirit takes over in his soul and prays in it and through it. At times, He will enlighten the person on a certain revealed truth so that he can understand it better, or he will become absorbed in deep union with God. At first this may last for only a few moments, but it will increase as time passes. The Holy Spirit will lead him to a love for the Mass, a longing for Holy Communion, a true understanding of the spiritual life, so that he views it from God's point of view and not from his own viewpoint.

When the Holy Spirit moves a person to see that worldly things mean little in comparison to eternal things, a longing for God then develops. Even a longing to die and be with God in heaven. It is usually in this state that the Holy Spirit gives His charismatic gifts, that is, the gift of prophecy, gift of miracles, stigmata of Our Lord, or the supernatural gifts. The Holy Spirit is not limited and He can and sometimes does give these gifts to those who are not really mystics. He can give His gifts to whomever He wishes, and whenever He wishes. Usually these gifts are given to the soul for the benefit of others. Nevertheless, they can be of great benefit for the person receiving them. We may desire to have these gifts, but we should let the Holy Spirit grant what He wishes, and act in us the way He wishes.

Death Of The Spirit, Or Dark Night of The Soul

One does not come to the mystical state easily; he must go through a further purifying process. He has to pass through the death of the spirit. This purification may take place in many ways, but it is always a passive purification in which God purifies the soul through trials and difficulties. It may come through illness, through a loss of friends, through misunderstandings and criticism, through persecution, through doubts against faith, or despair. It may be terrible temptations against purity. We have only to read the lives of the saints to see what they went through. The devil, too, will do his best to keep the soul from its goal of reaching spiritual maturity because a soul that lives a saintly life has tremendous influence for the salvation of the world.

All Called to Mystical State

Unfortunately very few people reach this state in life, yet *all are called to the mystical state*. Then why do so few achieve it? Some are misguided by the spiritual director, and that is why a good spiritual director is absolutely necessary. As St. Theresa of Avila said, the spiritual director should be a man learned in the ways of God. She said if she had a choice between a saintly director and an intelligent one she would chose the latter. The ideal would be to have a saintly and learned director. The spiritual director should be one to whom you feel free to speak about your spiritual life. You should go to him at least once a month to talk things over, and an hour should be sufficient to cover what should be said. Also obedience to the spiritual director is absolutely necessary. Some souls may get side-tracked in pursuing false spirituality, while others are just too fearful to live the spiritual life.

Spiritual Life to be Lived with Freedom

Some people, when they read about the spiritual life, spend much time trying to analyze the stage of spiritual development they have achieved. I feel that this is useless and foolish—a waste of time! We should learn to accept ourselves as we are, and just do our best to continue living our spiritual life in accordance with the Will of God. We should not worry and fret whether we are advancing, whether God loves us and is pleased with us, whether we should be doing this or that. We should learn to rely more on God and do all for the love of God. We do not have to constantly analyze our intentions, or try to figure out whether there was something sinful in our actions. We should live with the freedom of the Children of God and do what we think is best, pray in the manner we are used to, until our director advises us to do otherwise. We should also have patience and try not to advance faster than we should. It is foolish to desire to be a mystic, right away, when one is only a beginner. We repeat: the process of developing the spiritual life is usually slow and gradual.

Union With God

The highest form of the mystical state is reached when one has completely united his will with the Will of God. This union between God and the soul is called mystical marriage. This is a prelude to the Beatific Vision, and the union which all canonized saints have achieved. This does not mean that the soul is completely free from faults and failings, from temptations and sufferings. No one can completely eliminate imperfection from his life. That is why, when we see a saintly person, we can expect to see faults and failings. Because of these faults and failings many do not consider saintly people to be really holy. They think that they are only hypocrites or just ordinary Christians. That was why the sisters in Carmel did not realize they had a great saint in their midst. They said of St. Therese when she died, "What will they ever say about her? She was just an ordinary sister, and never did anything special." However, we now know differently. She did ordinary things with an extraordinary love of God. This was her secret to holiness and it can and should be ours.

Obstacles in Spiritual Living

When a man becomes serious about developing his spiritual life, he can expect ridicule and even persecution. His life will be a constant reproach to worldly living. When worldly minded people see the saintly person, they often strike out at him because their consciences reproach them and their way of life. However this should not discourage the saintly person because God can and often does use these things as an instrument for his spiritual development.

How often we act and react according to human respect. Many do not do what they should because of what others will think or say. We have to learn to live according to what God wants. We should never let human respect ruin our spiritual life.

Finally we have to be humble and not parade our gifts as if they did not come from God. Humility is truth and we must recognize our gifts and talents but always realizing that God gave them to us.

Pray Always

We all know that we can pray anywhere and at any time, but we should set some time aside so that we are alone. Sometimes we are moved to spend long hours in prayer and that is fine, if we are really praying from the heart and not giving lip service, or just putting in time to give the impression that we are holy. What good would that be? It is better to spend a short time in praying and pray correctly.

Each person has to develop the prayer life that suits him. We all should learn to pray always, no matter what we are doing or where we are. If we learn how to meditate properly, little by little, we are able to practice living in the Presence of God. We are able to see that what happens in our life is for a reason because God is with us; then life takes on meaning and we become fulfilled. God has a reason for everything that happens to us, yes, even sin.

God permits sin because we have a free will, and if we are humble He can use our sinfulness for our spiritual good. Why? Because we can clearly see that without His help we are nothing, that we can do nothing. It makes us more dependent upon Him. That is why He even allows great mystics to fall into sin sometimes, even serious sin. However, it is rare that a mystic will fall so low. No matter how far advanced in the spiritual life we are, we can still sin. Therefore, we should pray for grace so that we may always persevere in good.

Rosary

To help persevere in good, the Church has recommended other forms of devotional prayer. The rosary can be a tremendous aid in developing our spiritual life. This devotion has been recommended by many Popes down through the centuries, especially Pope Leo XIII and Pope Pius XII, who said the fifteen decades of the rosary every day. Pope John XXIII wrote encyclicals and meditations on the rosary, and he, too, said the fifteen decades every day. Pope Paul VI has repeatedly encouraged us to pray the rosary.

Yet, many do not pray the rosary because they say it is outmoded, old fashioned, a useless devotion. They claim that it is only monotonous repetitive prayer. However, we know that it can be a beautiful prayer if we pray it correctly, meditating upon the mysteries. The mysteries are based solidly on Scripture with the exception of the last two glorious mysteries, which are based on traditional teachings of the Church. When we pray the rosary, we should be thinking about the life of our Lord, or Our Blessed Mother, and Saint Joseph; we should be thinking about the virtues they practiced and try to make them our own. We can learn much about God and the things of God while praying the rosary. It is a prayer that can be said alone, but is an ideal prayer for families. As Father Peyton says, "The family that prays together stays together." We can also say that the family that prays together creates a better world.

Following are a few things we can meditate on while praying the rosary, and the virtues we can learn to practice.

THE JOYFUL MYSTERIES:

1. *The Annunciation*—The coming of the Archangel Gabriel to Mary and their conversation about the plan of God for mankind. Mary's reaction: her faith—believing what the angel announced to her; her purity—her concern about her virginity; her obedience—accepting the Will of God.

2. *The Visitation*—Mary comes to Elizabeth, and their conversation about the happenings in their lives because of God's designs. Mary's charity—coming to Elizabeth in time of need. She brings Christ with her, as she always does. Elizabeth's inspirational acclamation about Mary's greatness. Mary's humility—she accepts the praise of Elizabeth, but renders all honor and glory to God for doing such great things for her, and in her. She is truly Blessed and all generations will think of her in this way.

3. *The Birth of Christ*—Joseph and Mary go to Bethlehem to fulfill a civil law—therefore the virtue of obedience. Unknowingly a prophecy is fulfilled. The birth of Christ, the coming of the shepherds to the cave, the coming of the magi. The greatest virtue of this mystery is poverty—Christ's whole life was spent in poverty.

4. *The Presentation*—Taking of Christ to the temple, the offering of the poor. Simeon's prophecy about Mary's suffering, and Our Lord's future mission. The words of the Prophetess, Anna. The fulfillment of a church law—thus obedience again. We can also offer ourselves to God in union with each Mass being celebrated throughout the day—at each offertory.

5. *The Finding of Jesus in the Temple*—The discovery that Jesus was not with the caravan; the search for Him; finding Him in the Temple and the conversation between Mary and Jesus. Christ's return to Nazareth with Mary and Joseph and His obedience to them.

THE SORROWFUL MYSTERIES:

1. *The Agony in the Garden*—Christ praying to the Father to remove the suffering from Him; the interior sufferings of Christ. The invitation to the Apostles to pray with Him and their reaction. The acceptance of the Will of God the Father—obedience. The arrest of Jesus and the incidents that took place at that time.

2. *The Scourging at the Pillar*—We can meditate about what happened after the arrest; His imprisonment, His trial up to that point; the scourging and the exterior physical suffering He endured from that form of punishment.

3. *The Crowning with Thorns*—The things that happened before He was crowned with thorns, and Pilate exclaimed, "Behold the Man". The actual sufferings of Christ, standing before the people, being treated as a criminal. The derision and insults hurled at Him, and the cry for His crucifixion.

4. *The Carrying of the Cross*—Think about the remainder of the trial, His sentence to death, His way of the cross in detail, especially meeting His mother, stripping of the garments, and nailing to the cross.

5. *The Crucifixion*—the sufferings of Christ on the cross. The things He said, especially giving us to Mary as her children, and giving her to us as our mother. His death, the piercing of His side with a lance, and His burial.

At this point of our meditation we can unite ourselves with the Consecration at each Mass being celebrated throughout the world.

The sorrowful mysteries teach us much about suffering and love, for no greater love can a man have than to give his life for his friends.

THE GLORIOUS MYSTERIES:
1. *The Resurrection*—Christ rises from the dead. The appearance of Christ to the Apostles, the disciples, and to others. The things He says and does—especially giving the power to forgive sin, and His encounter with Peter. What the resurrection of Christ means to us—the victory over death, over sin, and an assurance of our own resurrection. The proof of Christ's Divinity.

2. *The Ascension*—Christ's last words to the Apostles; His promise of sending the Holy Spirit. His ascent into heaven to be at the right side of His Father in glory. The angels telling the Apostles to go about their business. Christ will come again.

3. *The Descent of the Holy Spirit*—The gathering of the Apostles with Mary and others in the upper room to pray and wait for the coming of the Holy Spirit. The coming of the Holy Spirit and the effects it had on the Apostles. The activity of the Apostles immediately after the coming. We can ask the Holy Spirit to come to us, and to form Christ in us. We can make a spiritual communion at this time in union with the Masses said throughout the world.

4. *The Assumption of the Blessed Mother into Heaven*—The life of Mary before her death, that is, from the time of the crucifixion and her death. The assumption into heaven, body and soul. Her entrance into glory and eternal happiness.

5. *Crowning of the Blessed Virgin in Heaven*—The Blessed Ever Virgin Mary, the Mother of God, Mother of Christ—the God-man, Mother of the Church, Mother of men, is crowned the Queen of heaven and earth, Queen of angels and men.

There are various ways in which you can pray the rosary so that it never will be boring or meaningless. Some like to think about the words they say; others like to meditate on the mysteries, or read some thoughts before each mystery, or read a short saying before each Hail Mary. No matter—if it is done correctly, it is a great benefit to one's spiritual life and personal **renewal**.

We have been speaking about renewal of the spiritual life through a personal commitment to Christ through Mary. We showed how this commitment will lead the soul to a life of prayer and the practice of virtues. We have also pointed out that this is to be a permanent commitment. But, how are we to be reminded of this in our day to day living in the world? I feel that this can be done through consecration of ourselves and our families to the Immaculate Heart of Mary. And since Mary brings us to Christ, through the enthronement of the Sacred Heart of Jesus in the home.

Consecration To Immaculate Heart

The story of Fatima is known throughout the world, even if the majority ignore it. Through the years, further revelations were made by Our Lord and Our Lady to Lucy, all of which are summed up in the title: "Message of Fatima."

The Message of Fatima stressed three things:

Rosary—five decades to be said daily
Reparation—by living a Christian life
Consecration to the Immaculate Heart of Mary

The request for recitation of the rosary was not something new. Our Blessed Mother had already spoken at Lourdes about the need for this great prayer. She also stressed the need for reparation at Lourdes. Our Lord made known the needs for atonement in the revelations at Paray-le-Monial, when He revealed the devotion to His Sacred Heart.

What was new was the call to devotion to the Immaculate Heart of Mary and the consecration to her Immaculate Heart. It was made known that it was the Will of the Heavenly Father that all the world be consecrated to her Immaculate Heart.

In 1940, Lucy, at the command of her spiritual directors, wrote to Pope Pius XII asking for the consecration of the world to the Immaculate Heart of Mary, including the people of Russia in a special way.

On the last day of October, 1942, Pope Pius XII consecrated

the Church and the world to the Immaculate Heart of Mary, including the people of Russia. Our Lord made it known that this act of consecration was incomplete.

In May, 1948, Pope Pius XII issued an Encyclical to the world calling upon every family and every diocese to concur in this consecration.

July 7, 1962, Pope John XXIII instituted the Feast of Our Lady of the Rosary of Fatima.

November 21, 1964, Pope Paul VI renewed Pope Pius XII's consecration to the Immaculate Heart before the entire Ecumenical Council and simultaneously announced a mission to Fatima by the Pope.

May 13, 1965, Pope Paul VI, through a papal mission, presented a Golden Rose at Fatima, confiding the "Entire Church" to Mary's protection.

May 13, 1967, Pope Paul VI made a pilgrimage to Fatima proclaiming its message to the world.

Vatican Council II has upheld the position of honor of the Blessed Virgin Mary and her role in the Church (read Chapter VIII of the document *On the Church*). She has been proclaimed the Mother of God, mother of men, and later, at the closing of the Vatican Council, the Mother of the Church.

It is our desire to fulfill the Will of our Heavenly Father in consecrating families to the Immaculate Heart of Mary; also to fulfill the requests of our Blessed Mother and the urgings of the Holy Father, Pope Paul VI.

Having made the consecration to the Immaculate Heart of Mary, we urge all to live in such a way that, through her, peace may be granted to the world, that honor and glory be given to God, that families may be sanctified, that is, truly renewed, and that we may be formed in Christ.

Enthronement of The Sacred Heart

Enthronement of the Sacred Heart in the home is a crusade to bring the whole world to the love of the Sacred Heart. It is an act of solemn, royal homage that is offered to the Sacred Heart of Jesus, the King of Kings, Lord of the world. At the same time, it is a solemn recognition of the Kingship of the Sacred Heart of Jesus over the home, society, and country; and an act of social reparation for all modern refusals to accept His Kingship, as shamelessly flaunted in godless legislation, godless schools, godless families. In opposition to such acts of "de-thronement," we freely choose to enthrone our King.

The core, the heart, the essence of the Enthronement is bound up in one word—love. It strives to bring into the hearts of men full realization of the love of the Sacred Heart for them, and to enkindle in them love for the Sacred Heart in return.

Active Spiritual Program

In order to accomplish this, the enthronement calls for an active spiritual program of three points: Prayer, the Eucharist, and Penance.

Prayer

We have already said much about prayer since it is necessary for salvation, for renewal, and for spiritual growth. The enthronement stresses a life of love, which will make a prayer easy and familiar. We pray as we love; prayer is simply an "exchange of love." The prayer we are speaking about in the enthronement is family prayer. There was a time when family prayer was common; the enthronement strives to make it so again. Thus we strongly urge family prayer. There are different forms of family prayer which we recommend:

The Family Rosary

Shared prayer—Begin the prayer with a song, then anyone who feels like praying a personal prayer should do so. The others are to listen, trying to make this prayer their own. They are not to interrupt or question what is being said. They are not even to discuss what was said during this prayer meeting. After the first one finishes, the next one may express his prayer in like manner. This continues until everyone who wishes to pray out loud has an opportunity to do so. At first, you will find much hesitation because no one is used to praying like this. Moments of silence, even long periods of silence, are acceptable. The more you practice praying like this the more you enjoy it and gain from it. One must always keep in mind, that when two or more are gathered in Christ's Name there God is in the midst of them. You can finish the shared prayer session with a song.

Scriptural reading and shared prayer—Sing a song, read a passage from Scripture, think about it awhile, then say what the passage means to you. Again do not ask questions, interrupt, or speak about it after the session is over. After everyone has an opportunity to say what he thinks, turn it into shared prayer as described above.

For daily family praying, you can also use the prayers in the booklet called *Family Prayer Renewal in the Heart of Christ* (Blue booklet) and the *Holy Hour Booklet* (Green). These two booklets have become very popular for family praying in the United States. They can be obtained from the National Center of the Enthronement, 3 Adams St., Fairhaven, Mass. 02719.

In frequent family gatherings for prayer, the King of love becomes a living member of the family. He shares in all the joyful and sorrowful happenings of the home, and by His constant Presence with the family produces that peace which is the source of Christian happiness.

Family holy hour is designed to make reparation in a spirit of generous love and penance for the fatal modern social apostasy of the home; for the sins of pride and sensuality of so many so-called "Christian" families. This holy hour should be made once a week, or at least once a month. It can be made together in a family group, or individually. It is to be made between the hours of nine in the evening and six in the morning.

Father Mateo, the Founder of the Enthronement in the home, urges the night adorers to begin their holy hour by uniting themselves in spirit with all the priests who at that moment are offering the Holy sacrifice of the Mass in some part of the world. He suggests that they pray for the following intentions: For the Holy Father, for the clergy, for those who have gone astray, for the dying, for peace, for the social reign of the Sacred Heart, especially through the enthronement.

Eucharist

The enthronement seeks to make the home a Eucharistic Tabernacle. It calls for frequent, even daily assistance at Mass and the reception of Holy Communion. The home thus becomes a Eucharistic shrine, a genuine Christian sanctuary filled with the Presence of Our Lord, for the members, living the Mass in their daily lives, bring the Fount of Grace which they receive in Holy Communion immediately into the home, to remain there while they live the Christian life. The enthronement of the image of Christ is a constant reminder of the abiding Presence of Christ. The two tabernacles of the Church and of the home are united by the common bond of the Sacred Heart of Jesus.

Penance

The third part of the Enthronement, Penance, is perhaps the most difficult because it calls for a richer type of Christian action. This is the doctrine of the cross. Before Our Lord chose the cross as the instrument of redemption, it was universally held as an abomination. It was shunned, despised, hated, the object of intense shame and infamy. But Jesus, in dying on the cross, sanctified it, enobled it, and raised it to the sublime heights of eternal glory.

Christian doctrine is this, that men share in the passion, the Cross of Christ, by their own individual sufferings, misfortunes, sorrows, and mortifications. They share in the cross if they accept these ills in the proper spirit and offer them as a sacrifice, which contributes to the salvation of souls.

Why Ceremony?

Like commitment to Christ through Mary and consecration of the family to the Immaculate Heart of Mary, enthronement of the Sacred Heart of Jesus in the home has a certain religious ceremony to initiate and stimulate its program. There are definite acts of what may be called devotion. These are helps. They are good, even in themselves. They are important. But in themselves they are not the enthronement.

In the most central place in the home, usually the living room, a table is arranged like an altar, with candles, flowers, and other suitable decorations. An image of the Sacred Heart (picture or statue) is placed on a table nearby with holy water. Guests have been invited. The entire family is present, if possible. The pastor, or another priest, has been invited to preside.

Vatican Council II, in the decree on *The Apostolate of the Laity*, stated: "The family has received from God its mission to be the first vital cell of society. It will fulfill this mission if the whole family is caught up in the liturgical worship of the Church."

And Pope Paul VI wrote, "Where, in fact, apart from churches and oratories, is the Divine Heart of Jesus more fittingly adored than in the sanctuary of the family? If the cult of the Sacred Heart of Jesus, King and Friend of the family, is thus nourished by liturgical worship, especially in the Holy Sacrifice of the Mass, personal and family devotion to the Sacred Heart (will become) a witness to the true faith, to sincere love."

Home Mass and Enthronement

This is the reason we have combined Mass in the home with the Enthronement of the Sacred Heart. The Eucharist was established in a private home, the Cenacle. What better place then, other than a parish church, of course, to celebrate the Eucharistic Sacrifice than in the "domestic sanctuary" of the home? These neighborhood Masses instruct people in the true meaning of the Mass, sanctify the family through the presence of Christ and His priest, and increase daily Mass attendance. When combined with the Sacred Heart enthronement the stress is on the heart of the Mass—the love of Jesus; His loving person; His abiding Presence in the home through the Enthronement and through continued family prayer.

Enthronement Without Mass

The enthronement is possible without having the Mass in the home, but then much of the symbolism is lost because when done with a Mass, the enthronement takes place after the homily.

Then the certificate is signed by the family and it is placed on the altar during the Liturgy of the Eucharist. The priest signs the certificate at the end of the Mass to signify that the covenant made between the family and the Sacred Heart is sealed with the Blood of Christ, through the sacrificial Eucharistic banquet.

Enthronement Without A Priest Present

The enthronement can take place, too, without a priest being present. Then the father, the head of the home, will preside.

Christian Life—A Way of Life

It would be no good to make a personal commitment to Christ through Mary, have the consecration of the family to the Immaculate Heart of Mary, or the Enthronement of the Sacred Heart in the home if these are just ceremonies for the time at hand. Rather, they are meant to be lived a whole life time.

We may not waste our time on externals; therefore as Christians we should have a healthy attitude toward statues, medals, candles, and scapulars. The Brown Scapular of our Lady of Mount Carmel (cloth scapular or medal) should be worn as a sign of our consecration to Jesus through Mary. There are many promises from Mary and the Church for those who wear this sign of devotion with faith. We must remember, however, that just wearing the scapular will not obtain the promises. It would be to no avail to wear the scapular and lead a sinful life. We would be hypocrites of the first class.

Superstitious practices and ideas must be kept from our lives. What good is it to have statues and relics all over the place, and live a superficial religious life? Why put our trust in a statue, a picture, a medal or burning candles as if these things were magical? Statues, banners, medals, relics, and candles are fine if we have a right attitude about all these things, if we know what they really represent, if we use them as God and the Church intend. These things must lead us to God—all power comes from Him. All glory and honor must go to Him. We may not use these things for show. It is what is in the heart that really counts—what we are in the eyes of God. Remember, you are nothing more or less than what you are in the eyes of God. You may appear great in the eyes of men and be a failure in the eyes of God, or you may appear as nothing in the eyes of men, but great in the eyes of God.

True Values in Christian Living

We have to maintain priorities in living our spiritual life. The Mass is the most important, then Holy Communion and Christ in the Blessed Sacrament. What folly, then, to come into the church and walk over to a statue to pray before acknowledging Christ in the Blessed Sacrament. Or, go to light a candle when Mass is being said. All the candles in the world would never equal one Mass. It is much better to have one Mass said for one's intention than to light a million candles. We must insist strongly—let first things be first.

Many people are puzzled about what they should pray for. We may pray for anything that is for our spiritual and temporal well being. Sometimes we ask for wrong or useless things, and God will never give them to us. Many times we do not ask with sufficient faith or perseverance, and then we think that God is not listening. He told us to ask, to seek, to knock; in other words, "be persevering in prayer." "To seek" is more than "to ask" and "to knock" is more than "to seek"—there is an ascending scale of earnestness here. Our Lord is telling us to pray with increasing urgency. But above all, we should pray as Our Lord did in the agony in the garden, "Not My Will but Thine be done."

APOSTOLIC WORKS

Eternal Life Gained—Love of God; Love of Neighbor

We are all familiar with the passage in Scripture where the lawyer comes to Christ and asks Him what he must do to gain eternal life. Our Lord answers him that if he would inherit eternal life, he must love—must love the Lord his God with his whole heart and with his whole soul and with his whole strength and with his whole mind, and he must love his neighbor as himself, and that if he did this, he would live—would live indeed, both here and hereafter. Love God—love one's neighbor—love oneself. This is the old law (Deut. 6:4-9; Lev. 19:18), and it is the New Law. This is also what the sixteen documents of Vatican Council II appeal to us to do—to return to the basic teachings of Christianity. They urge us to love God, our neighbor, and ourselves in a meaningful, positive way—to love as Jesus Christ loved.

We must never forget the first of these commandments—love God. Without the love of God, our love of neighbor risks being nothing more than natural kindheartedness, philanthropy, and even a somewhat condescending pity. Enthusiasm over and for humanity, if divorced from the love of God, is merely serving tables and filling empty stomachs. This form of love will avail nothing for eternal life (Cf. 1 Cor. 13-3).

Every One My Neighbor

Christ also answered the second question of the lawyer, "Who is my neighbor?" by using the beautiful and meaningful parable of the Good Samaritan. This question was the subject of much dispute in the time of Christ. The Israelites held the popular view that the "neighbor" was a fellow Jew, a natural descendant to Abraham. Some of the rabbis even limited it to a certain class of Jews.

The details of the parable of the Good Samaritan are well known to all of us. The man on his way from Jerusalem to Jericho fell into the hands of violent and bloody men. They stripped him, beat him, and left him half dead. A priest and Levite, seeing him, walked by. But then a Samaritan, a foreigner from a hostile race, came by. He knew nothing of the stranger except that he was from a nation which was hostile to his own and whom he was expected to detest. Seeing the man, the Samaritan was moved with compassion.

Who is my neighbor? Everyone in this world who is in need—everyone, without distinction of race or creed. And who is in need? Everyone on earth; many in need of the corporal works of mercy, and most in need of spiritual works of mercy. It seems that the world is one vast hospital, in which men are suffering from the consequences of original sin and from their own personal sins. There are the spiritual blind and lame, the spiritual leprous and dead, the spiritual deaf and dumb. These are in need, and each one is our neighbor. We must help them and we can help them in many ways: by our compassion and interest, by our virtue and example, by our sacrifices and prayers, by our service to them.

Christ—The Good Samaritan

We are all aware of how Christ loved us—each one of us is like the man beaten and left half dead. Christ is the Good Samaritan. He showed us in a perfect manner how to love, and whom to love—especially during the last day of His life. His death on the cross was an everlasting pattern of self-forgetfulness and self-sacrificing love. The message of the cross is the same as the words spoken by Christ:

> A new commandment I give to you, that you love one another; even as I have loved you, that you also love one another. (Jn 13:35)

Through sin we are beaten and left half dead, but the Lamb of God came to save us sinners, to take away our sins, and to give us life and give it abundantly. Christ, the Savior of the world, the merciful physician, by all He said and did during His life and death, was rescuing us from Satan and from all else that leads to misery. He came to purify, to heal, to nourish, to sanctify us.

He established His Church, of which the inn in the parable is a figure, so that He might provide for all the means necessary to heal the spiritually sick and to keep them healthy.

Like the Samaritan, He goes away, yet He makes all provisions necessary for our healing and health in the spiritual life till the time of His return. The two-pence given the inn-keeper symbolizes all the gifts and graces, all the Sacraments and sacramentals, the Holy Sacrifice and banquet of the Lord, the special powers He conferred on His representatives, the Pope, bishops, priests—the dispensers of His saving mysteries.

On His return He will repay us, for He often promised that no labor done in His name would be in vain. Christ, the Good Shepherd, the Lamb of God, will repay us all according to our love and sacrifice. (John 20:20-23; 21: 15-17; 1 Cor. 15:58; 2 Cor. 4: 7-18; 2 Tim. 4: 6-8; 1 Pet. 5: 2, 4)

> For I was hungry and you gave me to eat; I was thirsty and you gave me to drink; I was a stranger and you took me in .. Amen, I say to you, as long as you did it for one of these, the least of My brethren, you did it for Me. (Mt. 25: 35, 40)

Vocation To The Apostolate

The faithful, the People of God, are called to fulfill their apostolate in the Church, in the world; and the Church can never be without it. The activity of the laity should be similiar to that of the early Christians, which is clearly explained in Sacred Scripture. (cf. Acts 11: 19-21; 18: 26; Rom. 16: 1-16; Phil. 4: 3)

Christ founded the Church to spread the Kingdom of God throughout the world, that men might work out their salvation, and that all the world be brought into relationship with Him. All the activity of the Church to achieve this is called the apostolate, and the Church carries on the apostolate in various ways through all her members.

> For by its very nature the Christian vocation is also a vocation to the apostolate. No part of the structure of a living body is merely passive, but each has a share in the functions as well in the life of the body. So, too, in the body of Christ, which is the Church, the whole body, 'according to the functioning in due measure of each single part, derives its increase' (Eph. 4:16). Indeed, so intimately are the parts linked and interrelated in this body (cf. Eph. 4:16), that the member who fails to make his proper contribution to the development of the Church must be said to be useful neither to the Church nor to himself. (Vat. II, *The Laity*, 2)

Christ conferred upon the Apostles and their successors the duty of teaching, governing, and sanctifying. But the laity, too, share in the priestly, prophetic, and royal office of Christ, so they too have a role to play in the mission of the Church and in the world. They exercise this role by their activity on behalf of spreading the gospel to men, and by bringing the spirit of the gospel into the sphere of temporal things. The layman can do this because he is in the midst of the world every day. He is called by Christ to exercise his apostolate in the world as a kind of leaven.

A secular quality is proper and special to the laymen. It is true that those in holy orders can at times engage in secular activities, and even have a secular profession. But by reason of their particular vocation they are chiefly and professedly ordained to the sacred ministry. Similarly by their state in life, religious give splendid and striking testimony that the world cannot be transfigured and offered to God without the spirit of the Beatitudes.

But the laity, by their very vocation, seek the Kingdom of God by engaging in temporal affairs and by ordering them according to the plan of God. They live in the world, that is, in each and in all of the secular professions and occupations. They live in the ordinary circumstances of family and social life, from which the very web of their existence is woven.

They are called there by God so that by exercising their proper function and being led by the Spirit of the gospel they can work for the sanctification of the world from within, in the manner of leaven. In this way they can make Christ known to others, especially by the testimony of all life resplendent in faith, hope, and charity. The layman is closely involved in temporal affairs of every sort. It is therefore his special task to illuminate and organize these affairs in such a way that they may always start out, develop, and persist according to Christ's mind, to the praise of the Creator and the Redeemer. (Vat. II, *The Church*, 31)

Apostle Aided by Holy Spirit

To carry out the duties of the apostolate, the Holy Spirit gives to the People of God special gifts (cf. 1 Cor. 12:7), giving to each one as He wishes (cf. 1 Cor. 12:11). The faithful are to use these gifts for others (cf. 1 Pet. 4:10), becoming the good stewards of the manifold gifts of God. Thus they build up the whole body of

Christ in Charity (cf. Eph. 4:16). The believer has the right and the duty to use these gifts in the Church and in the world for the benefit of mankind and for the upbuilding of the Church. To do this, they need to enjoy the freedom of the Holy Spirit who "breathes where He will" (Jn. 3:8). Nevertheless, the faithful must act in communion with their brothers in Christ, especially with their pastors. The pastor has the duty to test the spirit, and to guide the faithful to use these gifts properly (cf. 1 Th. 5:12, 19, 21).

Program of Life—Union With Christ

The success of the apostolate will depend upon the living union with Christ. "He who abides in me, and I in him, he bears much fruit: for without Me you can do nothing" (Jn. 15:5). This union is brought about by a religious program of life whereby whatever we do in word and work is done in the name of our Lord Jesus Christ and through Him we give thanks and honor to the Father in heaven (cf. Col. 3:17). This program of life requires a continual exercise of faith, hope and charity.

Charity inspires us to do good to all men; to put aside all malice, deceit and pretense, envy and slander and thereby draw all men to Christ (cf. 1 Peter 2:1). Charity given by the Holy Spirit enables the laity to express the spirit of the Beatitudes in their lives. It enables them to follow Christ in His poverty so that they are neither depressed by the lack of temporal goods, nor puffed up by riches. They follow the humble Christ by seeking always what is pleasing to God and not seeking empty honors (cf. Gal. 5:26). They are willing to suffer persecution for justice's sake (cf. Mt. 5:10), and they are willing to take up their cross and follow Christ (cf. Mt. 16:24).

The layman should live his life and carry out the apostolate in whatever situation he finds himself.

> The layman's religious program of life should take its special quality from his status as a married man and a family man, as one who is unmarried or widowed, from his state of health and from his professional and social activity. He should not cease to develop earnestly the quali-

ties and talents bestowed on him in accord with these conditions of life, and he should make use of the gifts which he has received from the Holy Spirit. (Vat. II, *The Laity*, 4)

* The lay people who have joined various associations and institutes approved by the Church should adopt their spirit and spiritual way of life. They should also develop social virtues, such as honesty, justice, sincerity, kindness, and courage.

Mary the Example of The Christian Way of Life

The true and perfect example of the Christian way of life is the Blessed Virgin Mary. Thus we should commend ourselves and our apostolate to her maternal care.

> The perfect example of this type of spiritual and apostolic life is the most Blessed Virgin Mary, Queen of Apostles. While leading on earth a life common to all men, one filled with family concerns and labors, she was always intimately united with her Son and cooperated in the work of the Savior in a manner altogether special. Now that she has been taken up into heaven 'with her maternal charity she cares for these brothers of her Son who are still on their earthly pilgrimage and are surrounded by dangers and difficulties; she will care until they are led into their blessed fatherland.' All should devoutly venerate her and commend their life and the apostolate to her motherly concern. (Vat. II, *The Laity*, 4)

Lay Apostolate

The lay apostolate can be carried out either by individuals or by members of organized groups. The individual can carry out his apostolate by the testimony of his Christian life as he develops and grows in faith, hope, and charity. This is true, especially in places where Christians are scarce, or in places where the freedom of the Church is restricted. He can have a definite influence for spreading the Kingdom of God in his family, in the community in which he works. However, he should avoid two mistakes. One is to believe that a Christian life is only giving sufficient witness to others. And the other is to forget that man is a social being, and he must work to build community.

There are innumerable opportunities open to the laity for the exercise of their apostolate of making the gospel known and men holy. The very testimony of their Christian life, and good works done in a supernatural spirit, have the power to draw men to belief in God; for the Lord says, 'Even so let your light shine before men, in order that they may see your good works and give glory to your Father in heaven' (Mt. 5:16).

However, an apostolate of this kind does not consist only in the witness of one's way of life; a true apostle looks for opportunities to announce Christ by words addressed either to non-believers with a view of leading them into the faith, or to believers with a view to instructing and strengthening them, and motivating them towards a more fervent life. 'For the love of Christ impels us' (2 Cor. 5:14), and the words of the Apostle should echo in every Christian heart: 'For woe to me if I do not preach the gospel' (1 Cor. 9:16). (Vat. II, *The Laity*, 6)

The faithful are called upon to engage in the apostolate as individuals in the varying circumstances of their life. They should remember, nevertheless, that man is naturally social and that it has pleased God to unite those who believe in Christ in the People of God (cf. 1 Pet. 2: 5-10) and into one body (cf. 1 Cor. 12:12). Hence the group apostolate of Christian believers happily corresponds to a human and Christian need and at the same time signifies the communion and unity of the Church in Christ, who said, 'Where two or three are gathered together for my sake, there I am in the midst of them' (Mt. 18:20). (Vat. II, *The Laity*, 18)

Group Apostolate

The group apostolate is more effective than the individual apostolate because by united effort the community nature of the apostolate is expressed and fostered. The group apostolate is highly important and necessary because through joint action the members are sustained. The members come to be better formed in the spirit of the apostolate and thus more beneficial results may be obtained than if each member acts on his own. Each one should contribute what he can according to his talents, ability, and circumstances in life.

The purpose of the Apostolate of Christian Renewal is to develop one's interior spiritual life and to infuse this Christian spirit into the temporal order. The Apostolate is not meant to be an end in itself; rather it should serve to fulfill the Church's mission to the world. The dynamism depends on conformity with the goals of the Church as well as on the Christian witness and evangelical spirit of the individual member.

Apostolate of the Family

The most important group apostolate is the family, which has received its mission from God to be the first and vital cell of society. The apostolate of married persons and the family is of unique importance to the Church and civil society.

Christian husbands and wives are to be Christian witnesses to each other, to their children, and to everyone in the household. They are the first to teach the faith to their children by their word and example. They have the tremendous privilege of training their offspring for the Christian apostolate.

Christian couples have the duty to witness to the world by their own way of life the unbreakable and sacred character of the marriage bond, to affirm the right of the parents to educate their children in the faith, and to defend the dignity and independence of family life. Therefore, they, together with others, should work diligently to preserve these rights. They should try to see that civil legislation is brought about to assure proper housing, worthy education of their children; that working conditions be fostered for the benefit of society; that social security be guaranteed; that taxes be proportioned equitably; and that the right to live as a family be safeguarded.

Christian couples should provide active hospitality, promote justice, and do other good works for the service of all brethren in need. For example:

> Among the multiple activities of the family apostolate may be enumerated the following: the adoption of abandoned infants, hospitality to strangers, assistance in the operation of the schools, helpful advice and material assistance for adolescents, help to engaged couples in preparing themselves better for marriage, catechetical work, support of married couples and families involved in marital and moral crises, help for the aged not only by providing them with the necessities of life but also by providing them with a fair share of the benefit of economic progress. (Vat. II, *The Laity*, 11)

Service to Others: Unwanted Children

It is a wonderful thing to see Christian couples provide homes for abandoned and unwanted children. I am sure that many more could get involved in this important work of mercy. There are different ways in which this apostolate could be carried out, for example by taking care of young babies until they are adopted. I have known couples who took care of as many as forty babies over a period of a few years; others who have taken care of hundreds. Some could take children into their homes until the parents can take care of them again, or until they are old enough to be on their own. The latter could be done by families whose children are already gone from home. By taking young teenagers into their homes I mean to treat them as your very own—providing for their needs both material and spiritual; giving them a chance in life.

The child need not be a model child either. What about the child or children who get into trouble with the law, with a moral problem, or with a social problem? It would be much better to have a couple who is interested in them, who would help them to reform themselves than to push them into jails or homes of correction where they get little or no chance to reform. An understanding couple can do much good for people like this: listen to them, guide them, direct them, but above all give them a true understanding of love. Give them a chance to correct their mistakes and preserve their dignity.

I believe that there should be homes like this in every parish. I know it takes courage, understanding, generosity, and above all much charity. Why not think about it if you are in a position to give aid to such a child or children? If you do not have the resources then the courts could provide what is needed.

College Students

If your children are gone from home and you have rooms to spare, why not let young people who are going to college use them? Naturally, you will have to have rules and regulations, just as you do when you run any family. I think that the young people should pay something for the use of the room and meals, but at a lower rate than they would have to pay elsewhere. Young people need a break to get started in life, especially today. There are many deserving young people in our society who need this type of help. Maybe those who might be less deserving need it more.

Elderly People

The spare rooms could also be used to help the elderly people who have little or no income, or who are abandoned by their families. It seems to me that this would be much better than going to homes for the aged, where they feel abandoned and lonely. We all know that the homes for the aged are providing a much needed work of mercy, but often the prices are prohibitive for many. Also where they live together in a large institution, personal attention cannot be given as it should. The larger the institution the more one is treated as a number.

We have to treat people as persons. If a couple cannot take an elderly person or persons into their homes, they can at least go to visit them in their homes or in the homes for the elderly. While visiting them, it is easy to find out how they are doing, what their mental attitude is toward their lot in life and other issues of the day, whether they need food, clothes, or some form of recreation. It is important to show genuine interest in older people by listening to their complaints, or ideas; by giving them a motive for living and feeling worthwhile.

Many elderly people have the feeling that they have nothing to live for, that they are just waiting around for death, and thus they become self-centered, and while away their time in self-pity. They should be helped to see what talents they have and how to put them to use as a hobby, or even to assist someone in greater need. They might be able to baby sit, to provide for someone's education, to use the experience of life to teach others. There are so many things that could be done by the elderly to make life worth living.

Above all, the elderly could use their time to pray for others, even if the modern world thinks this is foolish or unnecessary. The world needs the witness of the elderly because they can show forth the virtues of a Christian life. Just as two married people who have been married many years give a witness to true marital love, how it has grown and deepened over the years, so the elderly can give witness to a life of charity for others. The lesson that is taught leaves a lasting impression, especially upon the hearts and minds of youth.

Charity Begins at Home

The family is the place where love, understanding, guidance, and discipline are to be learned. Anyone who gets involved in other things and neglects his family is deluding himself and not fulfilling his primary duty. The saying that "charity begins at home" is so true. It is only when one has fulfilled his duty at home that he is ready to become involved in other activities, organizations, or social issues.

How often we see people get involved in activities outside of the home to the detriment of the family. The welfare of the family comes first. We see some people make the serious mistake of becoming involved in too many projects. We see them go from one thing to another, dissipating their energies. They can never do any job well. It would be much better to be involved in one project or a few and do things correctly. Each one should evaluate the apostolate he wishes to become involved in, and then use his talent to the best of his ability so that much good can be accomplished. Many forms of the apostolate will be mentioned, but it would be the height of folly to think that one has to become involved in everything that is suggested.

Christian Education

I feel that the apostolate of Christian education is one of the most important and most pressing needs of our day. I strongly urge anyone who is talented and competent in teaching to be involved in this apostolate. We all know that Catholic schools are going through a crisis, mainly due to finances. We cannot expect to receive federal aid to keep our schools open, especially since the recent Supreme Court decision. Personally, I am glad that federal aid was not given in the form it was sought because interference from the state or nation with what is being taught in our schools would have been detrimental. Our school system could easily have been reduced to only secular education.

We are teaching or should be teaching Catholic principles and the Catholic faith to our children. If we do not do this, then it is better that our schools close completely. I do believe, however, that we should try to obtain tax relief or grants to the pupil so that he can use this money to choose the school he wishes to attend. In this way, there would be no strings attached.

Still the problem of finances remain. What is to be done? The people will have to sacrifice more if they want to keep our schools operating. It is not only the students' families who should carry the burden of running the schools, but everyone in the parish, or in the diocese. We all belong to the Family of God. We all have the duty to spread the Kingdom of God on earth. Many have the attitude they don't get anything out of it. Just think about it! Isn't that a very selfish attitude? Where is our charity? Where is our missionary spirit? Many say, let the bishop pay for the expenses of the schools. Let's be honest. Where is he going to get the money? Only from you—the People of God.

Finances of the Church

We hear it said that the Catholic Church is rich, that it has much property, and that it does not need any more money to carry out its works in the apostolate, or to fulfill its mission. However, this is far from the truth. What do we want the bishops to do? Sell the churches, schools, hospitals, orphanages, homes for the aged, and property for future development? Is that really wise? Through these various facilities the Church has contributed much to the spiritual and temporal welfare of the People of God, down through the centuries. All these buildings and organizations are necessary to fulfill the needs of many.

It may be true that some mistakes have been made in building some buildings or certain types of buildings. Maybe there needs to be better planning so that we get the most for our money, and that our resources be spent prudently. But if we were so foolish as to sell everything, we would soon find out that we would have to begin all over again and at a far greater expense. Maybe some of our facilities could be put to better use and we should make studies to see what can be done, then have the courage to do what must be done.

People do not know that most dioceses have debts or very little money in reserve. I agree that every bishop and pastor should make a complete financial report to the people so that they can see how much is on hand, how it is being used, what is needed for future development in the parish or dioceses and richer parishes help those who are less fortunate. This would be true missionary spirit. That is what has been suggested by Vatican Council II.

Fair Share Offering

People should give a fair share of their income to the parish through the Sunday offertory collection. What would be a fair share? I think three percent of one's income, and that means everyone. It would be admirable if people would give ten percent, remembering that God is never outdone in generosity. If everyone gave a fair share, there would be no worries about finances, nor would there be any need to have fund raising drives, festivals, candy sales, or dinners. The time saved could be used to carry out other activities beneficial to the Church and society.

Why do the schools cost so much to run? This year we have fifty three percent of the teaching staff who are lay people. Their salaries are much higher than religious teaching in the school system. This situation will not get better as time passes because fewer young people are entering the sisterhood, brotherhood, and priesthood. How to solve this problem? Maybe in time, more young people will follow a vocation to religious life, but for a period of ten or more years we will see more and more lay people getting involved in Christian education. Perhaps one way to alleviate the situation would be to have young college graduates give two years of their time and talents to Catholic education. They would have to be paid, but could they not follow a plan similar to the Peace Corps, giving their services for a minimal remuneration? It is something to think about and work to achieve.

Then, too, our schools have had to be updated and modernized so that our educational system could give comparable education to its students. This all has cost money, and it will cost more in the future. Nevertheless, it seems to me that any sacrifice, any effort is worthwhile to keep our Catholic schools open and operating at full capacity.

Purpose of Catholic Schools—Teach Religion

The purpose of Catholic schools is to teach the Catholic faith and bring the Christian spirit to the world. Religion should be taught in such a way that it has meaning to the one learning, and that it gives him what is necessary to live a good Christian life. Perhaps our approach to religion has been one of fear rather than of love. We have to continuously teach that God is a God of love; that He is a person who loves and cares; one who is interested in each one of us.

It seems to me that during the first six years there has to be a certain amount of rote learning in religion as in all other subjects, but it does not help to be just a parrot, giving back what one learns word for word. It is necessary that a child understand what he is learning and that it has meaning for his life. After sixth grade there should be discussions on various issues of our day according to the age level of the child. High school students should make an in depth study of Sacred Scripture and college students could get more involved in deeper theological questions.

If there were progression of learning in religion there would never be the boredom experienced by many studying religion in the past. I sincerely hope that the new directives for teaching religion will bring about the desired results, and make religion living for all. We have to use modern methods and modern devices and facilities to bring this about. Anyone who teaches religion should be well trained and have the qualities of being a leader. The dynamism of the teacher should flow into the class so that the students will be willing to learn more about the divine romance that can and should exist between each person and God.

CCD Program

Not all Catholic children are able to attend Catholic schools; thus we have Christian Doctrine courses for those who attend public schools. This program is important and must be even better presented than the religious program in Catholic schools. The reason for this is that the students have class only once a week for an hour, and in some cases a few times a year for several hours. New methods should be adopted to give a better opportunity to learn on a more personal level.

Instead of large classes meeting in the church or school class rooms, or church halls, provision could be made to have small groups study and discuss religion in various houses throughout the parish. Some parishes have done this with much interest and success. Even the best of programs cannot give adequate knowledge for living a deeply committed Christian life. It is necessary that the parents and members of the family talk about religion along with issues of the day, making practical application of Christian principles to everyday life.

Teacher Preparation

Leaders in the Apostolate of Christian Renewal could do much in this area. It is necessary that they train themselves adequately for the role of teacher in the Christian community. It would be advisable for them to attend training courses. There should be a class once a week for thirty-six weeks in methods of teaching religion and one for learning the doctrine to be taught. An hour should be devoted to each course. We need leaders for each grade level; early elementary—first to sixth grade; junior high school—seventh through ninth grade; high school level, and even adult level.

Christian education should not be limited just to children but should include everyone who can profit from the course. We need leaders on all levels of Christian education. I personally would like to see leaders use the knowledge they have gained from their courses by teaching on the level for which they prepared, by getting involved in home discussion sessions with neighbors, friends, and relatives. Much can be done if everyone qualified does his part.

It seems to me that Catholic college graduates are adequately prepared to give religious training to others who will teach to students on all levels. But where are our graduates? Why don't they come forth and do their duty? High school students going to Catholic schools could be used to help younger children learn their religion. It seems to me that we have a sleeping giant waiting to be aroused and become involved. We learn by teaching and this would be an excellent opportunity for our young people to feel the pulse of missionary work: If everyone who is in Catholic schools would become involved with teaching Catholic doctrine to others we would see a tremendous change in attitude about religion in our modern world.

Pre-Cana Conferences

Young couples who are preparing for marriage can receive much benefit from pre-Cana conferences. Competent lay people should get involved in this important apostolate, too. People who had experience in married life can give of themselves for the good of future families and thus help build a Christian community.

Every marriage has its ups and downs, and at times some people need special help and guidance. This can be given through Cana conferences, through counseling sessions, retreats, and discussions about marital problems. Every effort should be made to save a marriage, to build up love in a family, or to help someone in need in a marriage situation.

Permissiveness—An Amoral Society

We are living in an amoral society—a sick, mad, pleasure-seeking society. It seems to me that this comes from the philosophy of permissiveness that we have been following for the last generation, and also from the constant seeking for material wealth, power, and prestige. Little regard has been given to spiritual moral values.

In fact, Christian principles and values have been attacked from many sides; they have been ridiculed as something that belongs to the Middle Ages. They have been disregarded and cast aside because it is said that they restrict one's freedom, inhibit one's growth to maturity, or hinder development of one's personality. It seems that vice is considered to be a virtue, and virtue as something evil. That is why we have many grave moral problems in our modern society—divorce, artificial birth control, abortion, free love, abuse of drugs, crimes, pre-marital sex, abuse of alcohol, irresponsible driving.

The faithful are called to become involved in these moral issues, either as individuals in groups, so that others may learn what their moral conduct should be, so that they may have the proper ideas and ideals in moral matters, so that they may build a responsible character. Only in this way can we hope to solve these moral problems.

Divorce—Failure in Marriage

Our Lord was quite outspoken about divorce. The Pharisees asked him about this moral issue. Our Lord replied:

> Have you not read that the Creator, from the beginning, made them male and female, and said, 'For this cause a man shall leave his father and mother, and cleave to his wife, and the two shall become one flesh? Therefore now they are no longer two, but one flesh. What therefore God has joined together, let no man put asunder. (Mt. 19: 5-7)

By giving this answer, Our Lord upheld the dignity of marriage and declared that is was indissoluble. Apart from the moral teachings of our Lord, we know that whenever any couple obtains a divorce everyone involved suffers tremendously, and if they have children, the children suffer the most.

Toward Success of Marriage

Every possible effort should be made to make a marriage succeed. Many times we hear couples say that they do not love one another. We must remember that love is in the will. We can decide to love someone. Therefore these couples should make a decision to try again and again to love one another. It is a matter of wanting to make the effort to love. Love is not static, but should grow as time passes. There is no reason why the honeymoon atmosphere should cease. If one knows how to communicate with his partner, love should continue to grow each day, and there is nothing so beautiful to behold as to see an elderly couple who have loved each other over the years.

Communication

By communicating I do not mean a monologue, where one does all the talking and the other pretends to listen. I do not mean a dialogue, where one talks while the other formulates a denial of what is being said. This is not communication, nor good listening, nor useful conversation. Dialogue means that while one is speaking the other listens with heart, eyes, ears, and mind. He will see the facial expressions, hear the tone of voice, and really understand what is being said. Then when the party who is speaking finishes the other has the right and duty to speak and the other partner listens in the manner described above.

It would be a good practice to carry on a dialogue at the breakfast table, or some other time during the day or evening. This is most important in any marriage. One does not learn to dialogue overnight—it takes time and practice. Yet the effort should be made because it can make a marriage enjoyable, pleasant, peaceful, one in which love can grow.

100% Giving

We often hear that marriage should be a fifty-fifty proposition. Rather, it seems to me that the husband should give of himself completely, that is, one hundred percent, to fulfill his role in the married state. The same is true for the wife in her role. If each does this much, the marriage will be successful.

Danger Points in Marriage

There seem to be three points in marriage where troubles can develop. The first is when the first child is born. It can happen that the husband feels neglected because the wife has to give much attention to the child. The opposite can be true, too. The husband might spend too much time with the child. When the child is old enough to travel, where is the child placed? Right between the husband and wife, thus pushing them apart.

The second danger point comes after being married about seven years. Why? By that time the couple begins to take things for granted. A woman wants to be told that she is loved; she wants to be shown that she is loved. She wants to be held, to be kissed, to be told "I love you." If a man shows his love in the manner described, the woman will be happy and she will never be unfaithful. It is important that the husband kisses his wife before going to work and when he returns home in the evening. A man does not need such reassurance. He knows that he is loved by the way the wife acts, how she runs the home, and her interest in his and the family's welfare.

There is a physiological difference between a man and a woman. The woman is person-oriented, while the man is thing-oriented. He is interested in what happened; she is interested in who did what, what was said and by whom. A man may appear to be cool, blunt, inconsiderate, because he is oriented toward things. A woman appears to be warm, understanding, and concerned about the person involved. A woman is moved more by emotions, feelings, and intuition, while a man reacts more from cool logical reasoning. A man says exactly what he thinks, and means what he is saying. But a woman has other things on her mind—she tends to talk around the subject while the man is direct. I feel that if everyone would remember this physiological difference many arguments in marriage would be avoided.

Since man is thing-oriented he tends to forget the things which might mean much to a woman, for instance, feast days, anniversaries, birthdays. A woman remembers these things because she is person-oriented. It would be well for the woman to remind the husband of these important days. Then, when a gift is given, it should be something personal. It need not be much because it is the idea behind the gift that really counts. Just as when a young son or daughter gives you something he has made, it has great meaning even if it is really worthless.

The third point of danger in marriage seems to come after twenty-five years of marriage. Why? Perhaps there has been no real love present for a long time. The children are gone to take their place in the world so there is nothing to keep the parents together. We find that there are many marriages like this in which there is much unhappiness because they are trying to make a go of it only for the sake of the children.

A woman seems to go through a physiological change round the age of thirty. She feels that she is getting old and that she cannot please her husband. She may even feel that she is losing her mind. Understanding is most important during this period. The change of life period can also be a traumatic experience for both husband and wife. A man goes through a similar physiological experience when he is forty or forty-five. He feels that he is getting old; he might feel insecure about the future of his job, or about family problems. He, too, needs understanding at this point in his life.

Separation

Husband and wife are to work out their salvation together. When this becomes impossible, what should be done? In very serious cases a separation might be the answer, and this should be done with the permission of the bishop. A person should go to a priest to talk things over and decide what is best for all concerned. At times, even a civil divorce is necessary. However, we must remember this marriage is for life. Even if a couple is separated or divorced they are still married in the eyes of God and the Church. They may not remarry. This is not an easy thing especially when young children are involved. A person who finds himself or herself in a situation like this needs the Sacraments more than anyone. They should remain faithful to God—live as single persons. Carry their cross. Many will say that this is inhuman—did not the Apostles say the same thing to our Lord? But He did not change what He said.

Responsible Parenthood

The Church believes in responsible parenthood. By that I mean that the husband and wife are to decide how many children they can prudently have. This is not to suggest artificial birth control. We hear many humanitarian, and emotional arguments in favor of artificial birth control. We believe that this form of birth control is immoral—not intended by God. God gave man and woman the beautiful gift of sex to beget children, and when they use this gift in marriage they are co-creators with God. They are fulfilling their role as married people.

Population Explosion a Myth

Many articles have been written about over-population—the population explosion. Is the world really over-populated? Some countries are densely populated, especially in Asia, but there are many places which are under-populated, for example, Australia, New Zealand, parts of Africa, some European countries, Canada, some Latin American countries. And of course our own United States could handle many more people.

Surplus Food

We also read that many people are starving and undernourished, and that we cannot feed the world population. Is this really true? We also read that the world has an oversupply of food. A few years ago the miracle rice and wheat were discovered and these have helped greatly to feed the people of Asia. We have much surplus food in the United States stored in silos, granaries, and ships. We pay farmers a large subsidy not to grow crops on millions of acres. Why cannot the United States use this subsidy money, the money used to foster artificial birth control, and the storage fees to buy the food and give it to the underdeveloped countries of the world?

We talk about ecology, yet it seems that development of our resources and distribution of food are the greatest problem. Aid should be given, of course, in a way that respects and maintains dignity of the nation or the person helped. We have to help them with an unselfish motive, one of complete charity—not expecting to get anything in return or to meddle in their affairs. We have to help them to help themselves.

Thus new methods of agriculture should be developed and taught so that these people can become self-sufficient. Facilities for distribution of food should be established, especially transportation facilities such as roads, trucks, ships, planes. Charitable organizations could be used to distribute the food so that the poor and hungry will get it without going through the black market, or without much money being spent on high salaries to those administrating the program. If these suggestions were followed we would not have to worry about the economy being ruined or the balance of trade upset.

Artificial Birth Control

A nation that practices artificial birth control is weakening itself; is hurting its own economy. For example, it was reported that in 1970, we had eight hundred thousand less births than six years ago. This means that in six years less school desks, school supplies, and less teachers will be needed than we have now. Already we have more teachers than we need. Where will these teachers go to get a job? They have their degrees, but cannot use them. Later less homes will be needed—so you can see that birth control has an adverse influence upon the economy. To keep the economy healthy we need an increase in population. I believe that the nation that practices birth control is committing suicide.

Give Love not Things to Children

In the United States we have proposed legislation to limit the family size to two children. Penalties are proposed for families with more than two children. The state is interfering with the God given rights of parents. Talk about discrimination —anyone with a large family is discriminated against through social pressure, through government legislation, and through humanitarian arguments. We repeat that the parents are the ones who should decide how many children they prudently can have.

Many feel that they have to provide everything for their children. But is this true? They must provide food, clothing, shelter, recreation, and education so that their children can take their place in the world and have a good life. But it does not mean that they have to give them everything, including luxuries. This seems to be the mistake of the past generation. And what is the reaction of the young people? They are rebelling against this form of materialistic living. They feel they are not loved, that they are just given things.

We know that parents who act like this mean and want the best for their children, but the children will one day turn against their parents and say, you gave me everything but love. Children want love, understanding, guidance, and discipline. If they do not get this they will rebel and accuse the parents of not doing what they should. The family is very important because the health of the family unit contributes to the well being of the community, the nation, and the world.

Children should be taught to help themselves. This way they get to appreciate the value of money, and it gives them a sense of responsibility and personal worth. A large family seems to have a built-in training program for learning to share with others, to give and take so that they are prepared to enter the world. They become less selfish, more humble and charitable. They mature faster as persons because of the daily sharing in the family.

Natural Birth Control

We should not advocate that a couple have as many children as possible so that they become a burden to the state or community. The Church permits couples to practice natural birth control, which is the rhythm method, that is, not to have intercourse when the woman is in her fertile period. This demands self-control, but it is not an impossible situation. There may be cases where the rhythm method will not work because the woman has irregular periods. Still we may not advocate artificial birth control methods, since this is always objectively immoral. Many might say that practicing the rhythm method is too hard, but there are other times when intercourse cannot be had, for example during illness, or when one partner is gone from the home. We do recognize the problem, but it seems that not as many have this problem as we are led to believe. There are also many married people who have consented not to have intercourse. This is something they decided themselves to do as a penance, to make a sacrifice, to make reparation for those who abuse this God-given gift. I personally would never advocate such a policy for married people, but if God gives them this inspiration and strength to live this way—more power to them.

Unfaithfulness to Partner

We also find that many who do practice birth control are unfaithful to each other. Why? Because they feel safe—that they will not become pregnant, or that they will not get anyone pregnant. Wherever there is unfaithfulness love grows cold and many family problems soon crop up. They live in tension and a certain amount of fear. Communications begin to break down and often they become strangers to each other.

Abortion

Abortion is not the proper way to limit births, to correct the population situation, or to get out of an unfortunate difficulty. We believe that a person exists from the moment of conception and to take this person's life is murder—pure and simple. We rightly hear much about respecting the rights of innocent people, that we may not take their lives even in war. An unborn child, however, is the most innocent of all persons. Yet, we see people protesting against the killing in war and having no qualms of conscience in regard to killing a person in the embryonic state. Where is the logic in their thinking?

We see the rights of the unborn protected by laws of our land, by our own Constitution, and the United Nations charter. The unborn can inherit, and, if damage comes to a person in the womb of the mother through a third party, damages can be sought.

Again we hear arguments from humanitarian and emotional viewpoints. Yet, no matter how many arguments are used, murder may never be condoned. Where is our perspective? What kind of people are we? Are we not descending into a barbaric nation of the world when we permit this? We could very well see the day when our nation will cry out for more babies. It might come sooner than we think—perhaps in ten years.

Adoption

We should do everything possible to convince these people who seek abortion to have their babies and give them up for adoption. It is a wonderful act of charity for a couple to adopt a child. I know of one couple in Hawaii who have eight children of their own and who have adopted five Vietnamese children. They were not afraid of the sacrifice or worried about how they would provide for them. There are many people who would love to adopt a child. Many times our adoption policies are much too restrictive. Maybe an evaluation of present policies should be made and the laws revamped to represent a more realistic attitude.

Free Love

Advocates of free love say: use the power of sex anytime with anyone without any regard for the consequences that might follow. It does not make any difference to them that venereal disease has reached an epidemic proportion, or that many illegitimate children are born, or that abortions are performed to rectify their mistakes. They advocate that artificial birth control be used to limit the population. Anything is permitted as long as they are not limited in the use of sex for themselves. Pleasure for pleasure's sake is the rage in our day. Pleasure without responsibility. Yet, we know that even nature itself rebels against such an attitude. It strikes back; often leaving confused, emotionally disturbed people. Many times they cannot even face themselves and they turn to drugs and alcohol to drown their problems. They run away from reality and dream away their valuable time in a world of fantasy.

Sex Education

Perhaps our sex education has done much to instill this attitude in the minds of our youth. I believe in sex education if it is conducted in the proper manner. It should be given according to the age level; giving what should be known—no more or no less. It seems that we do not have sex education, but rather sex stimulation. More and more young girls are becoming pregnant. What is the real reason? Sex education should include the moral aspect, not just the physical and biological aspects. Parents should be coordinators in such a program so that they know what is taught to their children, so that they may supplement anything that was left out. We all learn by mistakes and we should be humble enough to correct anything which will be beneficial to the well-being of our own children. A realistic evaluation should be made to see what impact, for good or evil, the current sex education is having on youth. We may not bury our heads in the sand and say everything is fine when it is not. I feel that more emphasis should be placed on modesty and self-control. Immodest dress has caused much havoc in our world already.

Pornography

Pornography is another serious moral problem of our day. No matter where we go we see indecent literature on our book stands and magazine racks, in the movies and even on television. It is a billion dollar business and it is ruining the hearts, minds, and souls of our youth, and even older people. We seem to condone this. Little is being done to stem the tide of impurity coming from a greedy criminal element in our society. We even have advocates who say free reign should be given for peddling such filth and junk. We *do* what we *think*, and if we constantly see these things, read about these things, what will our thoughts be? What will our actions be? Can we really blame youth? Anyone who preys upon the passions and weakness of others has much to answer for. God help them.

We should be concerned about our young people and their modesty and the virtue of purity. Older people, too, often dress immodestly. If only they could see themselves as others see them. There is nothing so ridiculous as to see a middle-aged woman or an old lady act and dress like a teenager—mini-skirts, hot pants, slacks. They don't seem to realize that they have a natural beauty no matter what age they are.

Crime

Every year we see, from the FBI report, that crime is increasing in our country. Again, we can ask why? It seems that spiritual values are not being taught to our children. And many do not have anything to do. They become bored and seek diversion by committing crimes. Our youth talk so much about honesty and uprightness, yet more and more young people are getting into trouble with the law. They should be taught how to help others in need, to develop a hobby, to train their bodies through sports of all kinds, to keep busy in useful and constructive projects by joining the Boy Scouts or Girl Scouts, or another organization which is helpful to youth. There are so many things they could become involved in so that they would not have to turn to crime or drugs.

Drugs—Religion

The drug problem has become a national problem. We see people of all walks of life taking drugs. It is even down to the elementary school level. Some take drugs on a dare, others because they like it, and others because they get hooked. What can be done? It seems that the Jesus People have the answer. They are former hippies who copped out on religion, school, society and indulged in free love, drugs and alcohol—you name it, and they experienced it. Then they found Christ, and what a transformation. They found that they could do without free love, sex indulgence, drug abuse, and alcohol. They found that religion is the answer to their problems. Perhaps it may be a passing fancy, a fad, but they have proved what religion can do in one's life.

Why can't we try religion and religious principles, Christian values, to change the world, to solve the moral problems? Is it because we cannot see the forest for the trees? We know what Christianity did to change the morally corrupt world of the Roman Empire. We have to try Christianity again. It is the answer. We should give it another chance. Much is being done to solve the drug problem and we may not give up. We have to continue using everything at our disposal if we wish to salvage what seems to be lost.

Alcoholics

The AA has shown what can be done with alcoholics. They found that the person must want to be helped, and that only by accepting a higher power can they be helped. We have millions who have this problem; much time and money is wasted through the abuse of alcohol. We know that alcoholism is a disease and that treatment is necessary for recovery. Yet, the AA has proved that religion or a belief in God is the answer.

Irresponsible Drivers

Many deaths are caused by irresponsible drivers and by those who drive under the influence of liquor. We have fifty-five thousand killed on our highways every year and millions are injured through faulty or reckless driving. More Americans are killed in one year on our highways than have been killed so far during the entire war in Vietnam. More and more concerned citizens should work to bring about safer cars and highways and to see to it that laws are uniform and strictly enforced nationwide and even worldwide. For the safety of mankind we must shift our automatic priorities to give safety and economy precedence over prestige, power and speed.

Combat Moral Problems in Local Areas

In order to combat the moral problems in our society and to teach Christian principles we should work within our own parish, within our own diocese, and in cooperation with various civic organizations in the community. Some might feel that they can work on a national plane, or even internationally. Yet the work close to home is important, and if each parish, each diocese, and each civic community would make an all-out effort things could change within a few years. We cannot expect miracles or that problems will go away overnight. There must be a persistent effort by all over a long period of time. Never give up in doing good. The positive should be stressed, and all negative attitudes be dispelled. What good is it to talk about problems and do nothing about them? Get involved. Priests, brothers, and sisters should be leaders in guiding and directing the faithful, to encourage them to use their talents in whatever manner they can for the common good of the Church and society.

Neighborhood Emergency Unit

A neighborhood emergency unit should be established where a member can be called to help solve any problem that arises. Qualified people should be found who will give of themselves for the need of others. In larger parishes there should be no problem in finding people with the necessary qualifications. In smaller parishes they could band together and pool their resources in personnel and finances. Each could give something for charitable purposes. In this way the needs of the poor could be taken care of. The St. Vincent de Paul Society would be wonderful for this. Each existing organization should take a project and see it through, no matter what sacrifice has to be made. One has to have pride in the organization he joins and to do everything to achieve its goals. We will then see these organizations come alive within a parish, a diocese, or a community. The lay people should be led to give more of themselves, to become involved to help the needy and to work in charitable causes. Nor should their spirit be stifled; they should be given free reign to exercise their zeal.

The laity should accustom themselves to working in the parish in close union with their priests, bringing to the church community their own and the world's problems as well as questions concerning human salvation, all of which should be examined and resolved by common deliberation. As far as possible, the laity ought to collaborate energetically in every apostolic and missionary undertaking sponsored by their local parish.

They should constantly foster a feeling for their own diocese, of which the parish is a kind of cell, and be ready at their bishop's invitation to participate in diocesan projects. Indeed, if the needs of cities and rural areas are to be met, laymen should not limit their cooperation to the parochial or diocesan boundaries but strive to extend it to interparochial, interdiocesan, national, and international fields ... Thus they should be concerned about the needs of the People of God dispersed throughout the world. They should above all make missionary activity their own by giving materials or even personal assistance, for it is a duty and honor for Christians to return to God a part of the good things they receive from Him. (Vat. II, *The Laity,* 10)

Parish Council

To carry out the directives of the Vatican Council II, the laity should become involved in the parish council within their parish. Each organization and group can be represented in this council. Policies of action can be established, work assignments given; thus unity can be accomplished, and duplication can be eliminated. Much more can be accomplished by unity of effort. We must all learn to work together for the welfare of all concerned. There should never be any division or personal interest which would destroy what we desire to accomplish. We must be seen as a community filled with charity so that it can be said, "See how those Christians love one another."

Organizations

I hope that members of the Apostolate of Christian Renewal will join other existing organizations within the parish, the diocese, and the community. It is best for a person to join only one or at the most two organizations so that he is able to do his job correctly and efficiently. He should bring the spirit of the apostolate into the organizations he joins—the spirit of joy, peace, serenity, and love.

Be a Whole Christian

A whole Christian does not spend all his time developing his prayer life. A whole Christian is one who develops his prayer life and carries out activities in service to others.

Since the apostle in the Apostolate of Christian Renewal makes a total commitment to Christ through Mary and carries out his commitment by developing his interior life and giving service to others, he should make a special preparation. He should undergo a period of formation in whatever works of service he wishes to become involved. For his spiritual development he should attend conferences and seminars and make retreats. This should be an on-going process throughout his life. He should attend training courses for his activity in aiding others. There are many places where full preparation is being offered, so it is a matter of simply making a choice.

Lay Institutes—Damienians

Everything suggested so far can be put into practice by any and every Christian layman. But some, whether single or married, might want to make a greater commitment—that is, to take a vow of conversion of morals. Each member would remain in his home environment, being self-employed and self-supporting. We could call this group a lay institute. The vow of conversion of morals can be made to one's spiritual director, pastor, or bishop. I would like to call this group the "Damienians" after the great charitable apostle to the lepers on Molokai, Fr. Damien de Vester, SS.CC.

Perhaps centers will have to be established to give the training necessary for formation. Then, those who take this course will be able to go back into their areas to train others. They would become the yeast for Christian community in whatever work or living structure they penetrate. I firmly believe that training centers of ascetical and mystical theology are necessary because moral theology is not the guide for true Christian living. We have been bogged down too long in the principles of moral theology. Perhaps that is why so many are turning away from religion—it is too legalistic. It tends to curb the joy of living the true Christian commitment.

When one falls in love with God and catches fire with the zeal of the early Christians, he does live the principles of moral theology; they are evident in his life. And St. Augustine's principle proves true—"Love and do what you want." Augustine meant to say, you will do only what pleases God, if you truly love. You will be responsible, yet truly free. And you will experience the joy, peace, and love preached by St. Francis of Assisi. *This* is the goal one reaches by living one's Total Commitment to Christ through Mary in the Apostolate of Christian Renewal.

Make this prayer of St. Francis your motto:

> Lord, make me an instrument of Thy peace.
> Where there is hatred, let me sow love;
> Where there is injury, pardon;
> Where there is doubt, faith;
> Where there is despair, hope;
> Where there is darkness, light;
> And where there is sadness, joy.
> O Divine Master, grant that I may not so much
> seek to be consoled as to console;
> to be understood as to understand;
> to be loved as to love;
> for it is in giving that we receive,
> it is in pardoning that we are pardoned
> and it is in dying that we are born
> to eternal life.

Section Two

GUIDELINES OF THE APOSTOLATE OF CHRISTIAN RENEWAL

Purpose:

1. To give honor and glory to God.
2. To sanctify one's own soul and to help sanctify others.
3. To be of service to those in need.
4. To make prayerful intercession for the Holy Father, the bishop or bishops in one's diocese, one's pastor, associate pastors, religious working in the parish, and for the People of God within the parish.
5. To pray especially for priests, brothers, and sisters who may have a crisis in their vocation, faith, or any other problem.
6. To pray for those priests, brothers, and sisters who have left their calling and have returned to live in the world.
7. To make reparation to the Sacred Heart of Jesus through the Immaculate and Sorrowful Heart of Mary for the sins of the whole world.
8. To spread devotion to the Sacred Heart of Jesus and the Immaculate Heart of Mary.

Spiritual exercises:
These prayers are only suggestions and do not bind under sin.
1. Daily prayers:
   a) Fifteen minutes of meditation.
   b) Mystical Mass prayer.
   c) Chaplet Rosary of the Holy Spirit.
   d) Recitation of the Rosary (with family when possible).
   e) Renewal of Consecration to Jesus Christ through the Blessed Virgin Mary.
   f) Renewal of the Enthronement of the Sacred Heart and Consecration to the Immaculate Heart of Mary.
2. If possible, daily Mass, offered in the spirit of reparation.
3. Holy Hour in the home once a week (or at least once a month) between the hours of 9:00 p.m. to 6:00 a.m.

4. As a sign of one's consecration, wear the Brown Carmel Scapular or Scapular medal.
5. Make a retreat once a year.
6. If possible, visit the Blessed Sacrament daily for a five minute retreat.

Works to be fostered:
1. Foster fidelity to the faith, loyalty to the Holy Father, obedience to the Magisterium, and to the bishops as described in the documents of Vatican Council II.
2. Encourage Enthronement of the Sacred Heart of Jesus in the home (with Mass in the home wherever possible); night adoration in the home, in a spirit of reparation for the sins of the world; First Friday devotion.
3. Encourage the consecration of the family to the Immaculate Heart of Mary. Also family rosary, First Saturday devotion, Eucharistic reparation; wearing of the Scapular of Carmel or the medal.
4. Encourage others to recite the Chaplet Rosary of the Holy Spirit.
5. To be involved in service to those in need, that is, helping the poor, the underprivileged, the sick, orphans,. prisoners, the aged.

Organization:
1. You may join as an individual without forming a group.
2. You may form a group within your own parish; then, you would be the leader. Remember, a real leader gets others involved and gives them responsibility.
3. Send name or names of those who make the consecration to the national director.
4. Give a report once a year of accomplishments in service to others; how community is being formed in the parish, or diocese, or civic community. This report is to be sent to the national director.

Finances:
1. There are to be no fees or dues.

2. Each member will pay for his own books, booklets, newsletter, or religious supplies.
3. Any donation you wish to send to the national director to carry on the work of the apostolate will be greatly appreciated.

National Director:
Rev. Luke Zimmer, SS.CC.
Christ the King Center
The Apostolate of Christian Renewal
3 James Park
Los Angeles, Calif. 90007

Preparation before Joining the Apostolate of Christian Renewal

In order to become a member of the Apostolate of Christian Renewal we ask each one to make a consecration to Mary, to renew his or her baptismal vows, and to make a total commitment to Jesus Christ.

We ask each one to make a four week preparation before joining the Apostolate because it is a serious step. We do not want it to be something which is just emotional. We do not want people to join just for the sake of joining. The Apostolate is something to be lived. It is a commitment to become aware of what took place at our baptism and confirmation and to live that life with zeal and love. We are actually making a covenant with God. We are saying, "We are Your children and You are our God."

Suggested prayers during the time of preparation for Total Commitment to Jesus through Mary:

1. Daily Mass
2. Daily Rosary
3. Chaplet Rosary of the Holy Spirit
4. Meditation on the following:

FIRST WEEK: Knowledge of Self

1st Day—"God saw that all He had made was very good." (Gen. 1/31)
God said, "Let us make mankind in Our own image and likeness; and let them have dominion over the fish of the sea, the birds of the air, the cattle; over all the wild animals and every creature that crawls on earth." (Gen. 1/26)
God created us a little less than the angels; in His image and likeness; as King and Master of the whole world.
Therefore, we are greater than the whole world. He did this because of His love for us.
2nd Day—When we were baptized we became supernatural persons, that is we became participators in the very life of

God. We became members of the Family of God. We became children of the Father; brothers or sisters of Christ, temples of the Holy Spirit. Therefore, we are brothers and sisters to each other. Everyone is our brother or sister in Christ.

3rd Day—Our Father in Heaven should be able to say—"You are My beloved son in whom I am well pleased." "You are my beloved daughter in whom I am well pleased."

4th Day—To become a beloved son or daughter we have to put on Christ.

Do not judge others. (Matthew 7/15)

We should compare ourselves with Christ and no one else.

"I greatly admire Christ. I could easily be His follower, but I have never met a true Christian." (Mahatma Gandhi)

Am I a true Christian—an Apostle?

5th Day—An apostle is a committed person.

Commitment means to give oneself. It is a total gift that expresses the past, present, and future. It is a mystery which can only come from within oneself. This responsibility I can not pass on to anyone else.

You need not fear that you are unworthy to make a commitment. No one is ever worthy! *God chooses us first*—as a truly committed person I can effect the well-being of the whole world!

6th Day—"The reason why Christianity has not succeeded is because it has never been tried" (Chesterton).

"You are the salt of the earth; but if the salt loses its strength what shall it be salted with? It is no longer of any use but to be thrown out and trodden underfoot by men."

"You are the light of the world. A city set on a mountain cannot be hidden. Neither do men light a lamp and put it under a measure, but upon the lampstand, so as to give light to all in the house. Even so let your light shine before men that they may see your good works and give glory to your Father in Heaven." (Mt. 5/13-16)

7th Day—If we try to renew ourselves and become followers of Christ and live the life of a true Christian, we will have to carry the cross.

"If the world hates you, know that it has hated Me before

you. If you were of the world, the world would love what is its own. But because you are not of the world, therefore the world hates you. Remember the word I have spoken to you: No servant is greater than His master. If they have persecuted me, they will persecute you also; if they have kept My word, they will keep yours also." (Jn 15/18)

If we remain united to Christ we will bear much fruit—"Abide in Me, and I in you. As the branch cannot bear fruit of itself unless it remains on the vine, so neither can you unless you abide in Me. I am the vine; you are the branches. He who abides in Me, and I in him, he bears much fruit; for without Me you can do nothing." Jn. 15/4-5

SECOND WEEK: Knowledge of the World

1st Day—"Thou shalt love the Lord your God with your whole heart and with your whole soul and with your whole mind—This is the greatest and the first commandment. And the second is like it; You shall love your neighbor as yourself." Mt. 22/29-37; Mk. 12/30-31
Everyone is my neighbor and brother! Lk. 10/29-37
Love of Neighbor as yourself asks much—
—I will not deny anyone what I give to myself.
—This love eliminates all negative attitudes towards others.
—It is the beginning of the practice of justice.
It means to keep the Commandments of God. If we do this we show a great service to our neighbor.

2nd Day—On another occasion Christ said that we should love our neighbor as we love Him.
—To love in this manner, we will put the positive blue-print of Christian living into practice, that is we will live the Beatitudes.

3rd Day—At the Last Supper, Christ washed the feet of the Apostles and said: "This is My Commandment—that you love one another as I love you." (Jn. 13/34-35)
"Greater love than this no one has, that one lay down his life for his friends." (Jn. 15/14)

If we love our neighbor as Christ loves us, we are asking Him to love through us without blocking Him with ourselves. "I live now, not I, but Christ lives in Me."

4th Day—The summit of Christian love must be a mutual love in imitation of the Blessed Trinity in loving—

—Only Christianity has dared to demand such heights of love —to love with the love of God!

—Begin on earth to love and imitate the life of the Blessed Trinity. This love leads to the conversion of the world.

—Whoever has a heart full of love always has something to give. *That means You!*

5th Day—Love of God and neighbor must be positive and show forth in our daily lives. We do this by following the blue-print of Christian living: the Beatitudes preached by Christ in the Sermon on the Mount. Mt 5/3-12

Blessed are the poor in spirit—the meek—those who mourn—who hunger and thirst for justice—the merciful—the pure of heart—the peacemakers—those who suffer persecution for justice's sake—when men reproach you, and speak all manner of evil against you.

—In living the Beatitudes we also carry out in practice the corporal and spiritual works of mercy.

—*Corporal Works of Mercy*: Feed the hungry; give drink to the thirsty; clothe the naked; visit the imprisoned; shelter the homeless; visit the sick; bury the dead.

Spiritual Works of Mercy—Admonish the sinner; instruct the ignorant; counsel the doubtful; comfort the sorrowful; bear wrongs patiently; forgive all injuries; pray for the living and the dead.

The world is a vast hospital. We see the broken-hearted everywhere. Let us help them.

6th Day—"Amen, I say to you, as long as you did it for one of these, the least of My brethren, you did it for Me." (Mt. 25/40) As a child of God *you* are the hope of the world! Something to marvel at! The world needs you, your talents, prayers and sacrifices.

7th Day—"Let him who is greatest among you become as the least, and him who is the chief become as the servant." (Lk. 22/26)
Let us rejoice with those who do good, and have compassion on those who do evil.
"You have heard that it was said: 'Thou shall love your neighbor, and shall hate your enemy.' But I say to you, love your enemies, do good to those who hate you, and pray for those who persecute and calumniate you. Thus, you will be children of your Father in heaven, Who makes His sun to rise on the good and the evil, and sends rain on the just and the unjust. (Mt. 5:43-45; Lk. 6:27-38)

THIRD WEEK—Knowledge of Mary, Our Mother

1st Day—A young Virgin of 15 or 16 years of age is chosen to be the mother of Jesus.
"Hail, full of grace, the Lord is with you. Blessed are you among women." (Lk. 1:28)
—At Lourdes, Mary said: "I am the Immaculate Conception."
"...And behold, you shall conceive in your womb and shall bring forth a Son." (Lk 1:31)
"How shall this happen, since I do not know man?" (Lk. 1:34)
"The Holy Spirit shall come upon you and the power of the Most High shall overshadow you..." (Lk. 1:35)
"Behold the handmaid of the Lord; be it done to me according to your word." (Lk. 1:38)
The Holy Spirit formed Christ in Mary after she gave her consent. He will form Christ in us only after we give our consent.

2nd Day—Elizabeth was filled with the Holy Spirit and she said, "Blessed are you among women and blessed is the fruit of your womb! And how have I deserved that the mother of my Lord should come to me? For behold, the moment that the sound of your greeting came to my ears, the babe in my womb leapt for joy. And blessed is she who has believed, because the things promised her by the Lord shall be accomplished." (Lk. 1:42-45)
Mary could not keep her secret. Elizabeth recognized Christ in

Mary through the inspiration of the Holy Spirit.
Mary always brings Christ with her.
We will recognize Christ in her and in others through the inspiration of the Holy Spirit. Thus, the importance of being close to and open to the Holy Spirit.

3rd Day—Mary's reaction to Elizabeth's praise was one of humility. She recognized the gifts from God, and thanked Him for what He had done for her.
Read the Magnificat (Lk. 1: 46-55)
We should look into our lives and recognize the many gifts, talents, and assets God has given to us. Let us be grateful, joyful and peaceful.

4th Day—Christ is born in poverty—The Holy Family can identify themselves with the poor.
The angels sang—"Glory to God in the highest, and peace on earth among men of good will." (Lk. 2:14)
Modern man is searching for the God of his heart—but often he searches through emptiness, therefore he has a broken heart.
Many are men of good will. We must bring Christ to them.
The Holy Spirit will help them to recognize Christ.
—Let each one of us be open to the Holy Spirit and help others to be open to Him.

5th Day—"And your own soul a sword shall pierce, that the thoughts of many hearts may be revealed."
Mary was to suffer for the good of others. Christ did not spare His own mother from suffering.
Suffering has a place in salvation history.
What do I think about suffering? How do I accept it in my own life, in the life of my family, relatives, friends, the world?

6th Day—Loss of Christ in the temple. After finding Him, Mary said: "Son, why have you done so to us? Behold your father and I have been seeking you sorrowing" (Lk. 2:48)
"How is it that you sought me? Did you not know that I must be about my Father's business?"
Modern man has lost Christ. He will have to seek Him again. Where will he find Him? He should be able to find Him in *You*, a true Christian!

You must lead others back to Christ's Father's House where they will find the real Christ—in the Blessed Sacrament.

God is not dead as believed in the 1960's; He is hidden, yet those who seek Him will find Him. The 1970's are waiting for the resurrected God!

Will you help others to find Christ?

7th Day—At the wedding feast of Cana, Mary said, "Do what He tells you." And the water was changed into wine. At the Crucifixion, Mary watched her Son die. "Son behold your mother; Mother behold your Son."

Mary is our mother and she loves us dearly. She brings Christ to us and brings us to Christ.

We should live the rosary—pray the rosary—meditate on the mysteries of the rosary. Through the rosary we will learn much about our faith.

We should make a consecration to the Immaculate and Sorrowful Heart of Mary—then live it!

FOURTH WEEK—Knowledge of Jesus Christ, Our God and Brother

1st Day—Let us call to mind the mystery of the Incarnation—

The Second Person of the Blessed Trinity assumed a human nature from the Blessed Virgin Mary

—Therefore, in Christ there are two natures: One Divine, the other human. But there is only one person—a Divine Person. Therefore, Christ is God and man.

2nd Day—At Christ's baptism the Heavenly Father said: "This is My Beloved Son in Whom I am well pleased." (Lk. 3:22)

Who is Christ?

a) Who do people say the Son of Man is?" (Mt. 16:13)

—John the Baptist, Eliah, Jeremiah, or one of the prophets. (Mt. 16:14)

b) "Who do you say I am?" (Mt. 16:15)

—Simon Peter's answer—"You are the Messiah, the Son of the living God." (Mt. 16:17)

c) "Blessed are you, Simon-bar-Jona, for flesh and blood has

not revealed this to you, but *My Father Who is in Heaven.*"
(Mt. 16:17)

3rd Day—Christ was also a true man.

—Christ was a true man. He lived as a man, feasted as a man with the common people at wedding celebrations—He suffered fatigue and hunger.

—His own townsmen said of Him: "Is this not the carpenter's son?"

—the moral character of Christ was beyond reproach, and He revealed the tender nature of His heart throughout His life. He was kind, compassionate, and understanding of other people's pains and problems.

—Christ was a man for others. He became a true victim.

4th Day—The Mission of Christ

—His mission was to save others by dying on the cross; to take our sins upon Himself.

—He knew how He would die—on the cross; when He would die; how much and what suffering He would have to undergo. He predicted His own death.

—The vocation of Christ was to carry the burdens of men within His heart. We can readily imagine the inner sufferings of Christ which He bore all His life as a foretaste of His passion. His inner feelings and sufferings were openly expressed in the Garden of Gethsemane. (Lk. 22:43)

His mission was to be carried out down through the centuries. His message was to be brought to the whole world.

5th Day—Christ established His Church, which is a gift of the Divine Love of His Sacred Heart through the coming of the Holy Spirit.

—Christ established a hierarchical church, not a democratic church.

—Peter was chosen by the Father to be the head of the Church— since He revealed to Peter who Christ was.

—Then Christ said: "And I say to you, you are Peter, and upon this rock I will build My Church, and the gates of hell shall not prevail against it."

—Peter was far from being a rock. Therefore, Christ was referring to the Primacy of Peter.

—The Pope is the true successor of Peter, and the bishops are successors of the Apostles.
—Love the Pope, the bishops, priests, religious and pray for them.

6th Day—The mission of the Church

"Go, therefore, and make disciples of all nations, baptizing them in the name of the Father, and of the Son, and of the Holy Spirit, *teaching* them *to observe all* that I have commanded you; and behold, I am with you all days, even unto the consummation of the world.

—You are the Church. Therefore, you have to preach Christ and His message. You also have to live His message.

—Remember, you are what you are in the sight of God; nothing more and nothing less!

—In order to live His message, you should make a total commitment to Christ; making a convenant with Him. This should be done also in your family circle, in your domestic church, which is your home by having the Enthronement of the Sacred Heart of Jesus.

7th Day—A committed Christian loves his Church, upholds the faith as taught by the Church, and does everything he can to spread the message of Christ.

—He lives his faith by going to the Sacraments, by praying, by giving loving service to his neighbor.

—Remember, you will learn more about your total commitment through living the Christian life.

Let this be our motto: "Lord, give me the serenity to accept the things I cannot change (other people's minds and personality)—Your Territory! The courage to change the things I can (my own weaknesses, faults, and failings)—My Territory! The Wisdom to know the difference (between Your territory and mine)."

B) *Ceremony for the Total Commitment* to Jesus Christ through the Blessed Virgin Mary (Without Mass)

1. Hymn suitable for the occasion

2. Talk by the priest or the one presiding
3. Suitable Hymn
4. Consecrants read the prayer of commitment:

In the presence of the heavenly court, I, N. . . . , choose you today as my mother. I deliver and consecrate myself to you completely; my body and soul, my goods, both interior and exterior, and even the value of all my good actions, past, present, and future.

I also renew and ratify today in your hands, O Immaculate Mother, the vows of my baptism; I renounce forever Satan, his pomps and works.

Through your hands, O Blessed Mother, I consecrate and commit myself entirely to Jesus Christ your Son and my Brother, to carry my cross after Him all the days of my life, and to be more faithful to Him than ever before.

Grant that I be faithful in living this commitment every day of my life. Amen.

5. The one presiding:

My brothers and sisters, may Almighty God bless you and keep you faithful to your commitment to Jesus through Mary.

6. Suitable Hymn

C) *Ceremony for the Total Commitment* to Jesus Christ through the Blessed Virgin (With the Mass)

1. Entrance Song
2. Greeting prayer, Penitential Rite, Litany of Mercy
3. Glory to God
4. First Scriptural Reading and Response
5. Second Scriptural Reading and Gospel Acclamation
6. Gospel
7. Homily
8. Creed (if no creed, the Apostles' Creed).
9. Prayer of intercession.
10. Offertory Hymn and Procession
11. Commitment Ceremony:

Consecrants Read the Prayer of Commitment:

In the presence of the heavenly court, I, N...., choose you today as my mother. I deliver and consecrate myself to you completely; my body and soul, my goods, both interior and exterior, and even the value of all my good actions, past, present, and future.

I also renew and ratify today in your hands, O Immaculate Mother, the vows of my baptism; I renounce forever Satan, his pomps and works.

Through your hands, O Blessed Mother, I consecrate and commit myself entirely to Jesus Christ, your Son and my Brother, to carry my cross after Him all the days of my life, and to be more faithful to Him than ever before.

Grant that I may be faithful in living my commitment every day of my life. Amen.

12. Holy, Holy, Holy, The Our Father, the Lamb of God may be sung.
13. Communion Hymn
14. Priest presiding says:

My brothers and sisters, may Almighty God bless you and help you to keep your commitment to Jesus through Mary.

15. Finish the Mass and end with a suitable Hymn.

Consecration of the Family to the Immaculate Heart of Mary

Blessing of the Home
Priest: Peace be to this house.
R: And to all who dwell herein.
Priest: Sprinkle me, O Lord, with hyssop, and I shall be purified; wash me and I shall be whiter than snow. Have mercy on me, O God, in Your mercy. Glory be to the Father and to the Son and to the Holy Spirit.
R: As it was in the beginning, is now, and ever shall be, world without end. Amen.
Priest: Sprinkle me, O Lord, with hyssop, and I shall be purified; wash me and I shall be whiter than snow.
V. O Lord, hear my prayer. R. And let my cry come to you.
V. The Lord be with you. R. And also with you.

Let us pray:

Hear us, Lord, Holy Father, Almighty and Eternal God, and graciously send Your holy angel from heaven to watch over, to cherish, to protect, to abide with, and to defend all who dwell in this house. Through Christ Our Lord.   R. Amen.

Solemn Blessing of the image of the Blessed Virgin Mary
P. Our help is in the name of the Lord.
All: Who made heaven and earth.
P. The Lord be with you.
All: And also with you.

Let us Pray:

Almighty and everlasting God, You do not forbid us to carve or paint likenesses of Your saints, in order that whenever we look at them with our bodily eyes we may call to mind their holy lives, and resolve to follow in their footsteps; may it please You to bless and to hallow this statue (or picture), which has been made in memory and honor of the Blessed Virgin Mary, Mother of our Lord Jesus Christ, and grant that all who in its presence pay devout homage to the Blessed Virgin may by her merits and intercession obtain Your grace in this life and everlasting glory in the life to come, through Christ our Lord.
All: Amen.

The image is sprinkled with holy water (Roman Ritual).
Act of Consecration of the family to the Immaculate Heart of Mary. (Begun by father or mother, said by all)

Queen of the most Holy Rosary, and tender Mother of men,/ to fulfill the desires of the Sacred Heart,/ and the request of the Vicar of your Son on earth,/ we consecrate ourselves to you, and to your Immaculate Heart,/ and recommend to you,/ all the families of our nation, and the world.

Please accept our consecration, dearest Mother,/ and use us and all families as you wish,/ to accomplish your designs upon the world.

O Immaculate Heart of Mary,/ Queen of heaven and earth, and of our family,/ rule over us, together with the Sacred Heart of Jesus Christ, our King.

Save us from the spreading flood of modern paganism,/ kindle in our hearts and homes the love of purity,/ the practice of the Christian life, and an ardent zeal for souls, and for the holiness of family life.

We come with confidence to you,/ O Throne of Grace and Mother of Fair Love;/ inflame us with the same Divine fire which has inflamed your own Immaculate Heart.

Make our hearts and homes your shrine,/ and through us make the Heart of Jesus/ rule and triumph in every family in the world. Amen.

Our Father, Hail Mary, Glory Be—for the intentions of the Holy Father.
All:

Hail, Queen and Mother of mercy, hail, our life, comfort, and hope. Exiled sons of Eve, with loud voice we call upon you. As we journey in sorrow and lament through this valley of tears, we sigh and long for your help. Come then, our advocate, and turn those eyes of pity towards us now. When this time of exile is past, show us Jesus, the blessed Fruit of your womb, gentle, loving and kind Virgin Mary.

P: Pray for us, Holy Mother of God.
All: Make us worthy of the promises of Christ.

Enthronement of the Sacred Heart of Jesus in the home— (with Mass in the home)

Entrance Hymn
Petitions (by Celebrant):
1. For all the times we have failed to recognize Christ as the Head of our families. All: Lord, have mercy.
2. For all the times we have hurt one another with our words and acts. All: Lord, have mercy.
3. For all the times we have refused to forgive those who have offended us. All: Lord, have mercy.
4. For all the times we have been selfish and inconsiderate of others. All: Christ, have mercy.
5. For all the times we have given bad example to our neighbors. All: Christ, have mercy.
6. For all the times we have failed to see Christ in one another. All: Christ, have mercy.
7. For all the times we have been lazy in performing our duties. All: Lord, have mercy.
8. For all the times we have spoken uncharitably about others. All: Lord, have mercy.
9. For all the times we have lacked the courage to be truly committed Christians. All: Lord, have mercy.

Gloria.
First Scriptural reading: 1 John 4: 7-12.
Scriptural response: (Gradual).
Gospel: Matt. 11:25-30.
Homily.
Enthronement ceremony after the Homily— *Blessing of the image* —held by the father of the family.
Priest: Our help is in the name of the Lord.
   All: Who made heaven and earth.
Priest: The Lord be with you.
   All: And also with you.
Priest: Let us pray:
   Almighty, everlasting God, Who approves the painting and sculpturing of the image of Your saints, so that as often as we gaze upon them we are reminded to imitate their deeds, bless and

sanctify this image made in honor and in memory of the most Sacred Heart of Your only begotten Son, Our Lord Jesus Christ; and grant that whoever in its presence humbly strives to serve and honor the Sacred Heart of Your only begotten Son, may obtain through His merits and intercession grace in this life and everlasting glory in the world to come. Amen.

(Image is sprinkled with holy water.)

Enthronement of the image by the father of the family.
(If possible, the picture or statue of the Sacred Heart should be enthroned in back of the altar which is facing the people so that all can see during the Mass. Otherwise in a conspicuous place.)
Creed—If the Creed is not said during the Mass, all now recite the Apostles' Creed as an act of faith and reparation.

The Apostles' Creed

I believe in God, the Father Almighty, Creator of heaven and earth; and in Jesus Christ, His only Son, Our Lord; Who was conceived by the Holy Spirit, born of the Virgin Mary, suffered under Pontius Pilate, was crucified, died and was buried. He descended into hell; the third day He rose again from the dead. He ascended into heaven, sits at the right hand of God, the Father Almighty; from there He shall come to judge the living and the dead.

I believe in the Holy Spirit, the Holy Catholic Church, the communion of Saints, the forgiveness of sins, the resurrection of the body and life everlasting. Amen.

Act of Consecration as follows:
Almighty and Eternal Father, we the .... family (each member of the family says his first name beginning with the father) consecrate ourselves and our home to the Sacred Heart of Your only begotten Son Who loves us with a tender and everlasting love. May we return this love as He comes into the midst of our family to live and share our life in a special way from this day on.

We accept you, Divine Heart of Jesus, as our loving King and member of this family. Stay with us, Lord. Sanctify our joys and comfort us in all our sorrows. May Your Holy Spirit penetrate each of us that we may be continually aware of Your special Presence among us, especially in one another. Help us through this consecration to have a deep and loving respect for one another so that we may daily live this consecration in our family life.

Let our love go beyond our home into the world so that we may do our part to win other families to Your Sacred Heart; thus helping to form a real community among the families of this parish and of the whole world.

All: Sacred Heart of Jesus, we love You.
> Sacred Heart of Jesus, Thy Kingdom come!
> Immaculate Heart of Mary, pray for us.
> St. Joseph, pray for us!
> St. Margaret Mary, pray for us!
> Glory to the Sacred Heart of Jesus forever and ever. Amen.

Covenant—Signing of the Certificate by the father, mother, and children (the priest signs at the end of the Mass.)

Suggested prayer of intercession:
Introductory prayer (Celebrant):

Lord Jesus, You have told us, "Whatever you ask the Father in My name, He will give it to you," grant this family the petitions which they are about to present to Your Father in Your Name.

Father:

That the Sacred Heart of Jesus may be known and loved in a special way in our home, in our parish, and throughout the world. We pray to the Lord. All: Lord, hear our prayer.

Mother:

That our family may keep alive the spirit of our enthronement by gathering daily to renew our consecration, we pray to the Lord. All: Lord, hear our prayer.

Children:

For all the members of our family, we pray to the Lord. All: Lord, hear our prayer.

Family:

That we may ever give thanks to God for choosing our family to receive the gift of His presence and love, we pray to the Lord.

That our Enthronement shrine may ever remind us that Christ is King of our family, we pray to the Lord.

That God may bless our family with vocations to the priesthood and religious life, we pray to the Lord.

That each member of this family may have a deep and living faith through frequent celebration of the Eucharist together, we pray to the Lord.

That our Blessed Mother and St. Joseph intercede for us that our family life may be based on that of the Holy Family, we pray to the Lord.

That the Enthronement may be known, understood, and requested in our parish community, we pray to the Lord.

Celebrant:

Sacred Heart of Jesus, You have promised to bless in a special way those families who honor Your Divine Heart in their homes. Please shower Your blessings on this family which has invited You to preside over it as its King and to abide with it as its friend. In Your Eucharistic sacrifice we are about to offer, through You, with You, and in You, please present all our petitions to Your loving Father. Amen.

The signed certificate is carried to the altar during the Offertory Procession.

Offertory Prayer and Hymn.

Communion Prayer and Hymn.

At the end of the Mass all say:

"The Lord shall be enthroned as King forever; the Lord shall bless His people with Peace." (Ps. 28)

The priest signs the "Covenant."

Recessional Hymn:

HEART OF JESUS, KING AND SAVIOR
(Melody—Tantum Ergo: do, re, mi, do)

Heart of Jesus, King and Savior,
Hear our prayer—Thy Kingdom come!
In our family, school and parish

Be our friend, our King of love.
Through Your Eucharistic Banquet
Make our hearts unite as one.

God the Father, Our Creator.
Loved us so, He gave His Son.
See the Crib, the Cross, the Altar,
Proofs of love for everyone.
Heart of Jesus, send Your Spirit.
Love's repaid by love alone.

Heart of Jesus, King and Brother,
In our home set up Your Throne.
Share our every joy and sorrow.
You we love and You alone.
Help us truly love our neighbor.
Make love reign in heart and home!

By Fr. Francis Larkin, SS.CC.
Imprimatur: Archbishop Thomas McDonough
Liturgical Committee

Family "Do It Yourself" Enthronement Ritual

Our Family Enthrones the Sacred Heart of Jesus as Our King, Provider and Friend.

(All are seated while the father—or in his absence, mother—explains what is about to take place.)

Father: "You know, I think this might well be one of the most important gatherings of our life. The reason I say this is because I'm convinced from what we have been told and what I've read about the Enthronement, it brings terrific blessings to families. And the good Lord knows we need them.

"Actually what we are doing today is to invite Jesus to come into our home and to give Him a free hand. And we won't have to worry about what He does because He is the only One Who knows what He is doing and whatever He does is for our good, for He is the only One Who truly loves us and is our loyal and powerful Friend.

"By the Enthronement, we are told, we enthrone Jesus as our King who rules over us through love—more like a Father than a ruler. He takes charge of all our affairs, big and small. He becomes our generous Provider, our family Friend, our spiritual Physician, our financial Advisor, our life Insurer, our heavenly Banker, our constant Companion, the unseen Guest at every meal.

"And we want Him to be all these things because each and every one of us needs His help. It isn't easy to be good. We can't do it alone, but with Jesus' help we can make it.

"Isn't it wonderful to think that Jesus will be a real member of our family from now on? He comes into our home, not because we are better than anyone else, but because He knows how much we need Him. But if we expect Jesus to bless us, we have to promise to try harder to be good—to God, to each other and to those we meet outside of our home.

"We hope that by what we are going to do today, and by the way we think of Jesus and talk to Him and trust Him in the future, that we will make up for so many families and so many people who don't love Jesus and are offending Him."

The Enthronement Ceremony

1. Father: Now let us all stand while in your name I enthrone the Sacred Heart as the Head of our family.
(All gather around the father, who takes the Sacred Heart image and slowly walks over to the place prepared for it and enthrones it, that is, puts it on the "throne").
All: Jesus, You are the King and Friend of our family. We accept Your loving rule over us. Stay with us as our best Friend. We need You.
Father: Now we are going to say the Apostles' Creed to make up for a lot of people we know who don't believe or practice what Jesus taught.

2. The Apostles' Creed.
Father: Today we are going to turn our family over to the Sacred Heart of Jesus. When we were baptized we were dedicated to God. That's what we are going to do now—renew our dedication to God by consecrating ourselves to His loving Heart.

3. Act of Consecration.
Almighty and Eternal Father,/ we the (Smith) family,/ (then each member of the family says his first name beginning with the father) consecrate ourselves and our home to the Sacred Heart of Your only begotten Son/ Who loves us with a tender and everlasting love./ May we return this love as He comes into the midst of our family/ to live and share our life in a special way from this day on.

We accept You, Divine Heart of Jesus,/ as a living member of this family./ Stay with us, Lord,/ Sanctify our joys and comfort us in all our sorrows./ May Your Holy Spirit inspire each of us/ so that we may be continually aware of Your presence among us,/ especially in one another./ Help us, through this consecration,/ to have a deep and loving respect for one another./ So that we may daily live this consecration in our family life.

Let our love go beyond our home into the world/ so that we may do our part/ to win other families to Your Sacred Heart./ Thus helping to form a real community among the families of this parish/ and of the whole world.
All: Sacred Heart of Jesus, we love You, Sacred Heart of Jesus

Thy Kingdom Come! Immaculate Heart of Mary, Pray for us. St. Joseph, Pray for us. St. Margaret Mary, Pray for us. Glory to the Sacred Heart of Jesus forever and ever. Amen.

4. Short Prayer of the Faithful

Father: That the Sacred Heart of Jesus may be known and loved and served in a special way, in our home, in our neighborhood and in our parish, we pray to the Lord. Lord, hear our prayer.

Mother: That Mary, our Mother, through her Immaculate Heart, help us keep alive the spirit of our Enthronement by bringing us together daily to pray in the Name of Jesus, let us pray to the Lord: Lord, hear our prayer.

Children (or Parents): For all the members of our family who are not with us today, both living and dead, let us pray to the Lord: Lord hear our prayer!

All: That God may bless our family with vocations to the priesthood and religious life, let us pray to the Lord.

(Note: Personal requests may be added, if desired)

5. Litany of Thanksgiving

Father: Just as we thank God our heavenly Father, through Jesus, His Son, during the Mass, so also now we thank the Sacred Heart of Jesus, through the Heart of His Mother.

Mother: For giving us our children.

All: We thank You, Lord.

Children: For giving us our parents.

All: We thank You, Lord.

Father: For coming to our home.

All: We thank You, Lord.

Mother: For giving us Mary, Your Mother, as our Mother.

All: We thank You, Lord.

Children: For our Holy Father, the Pope, our Bishop, our priests, our sisters and teachers.

All: We thank You, Lord.

Father: Now if there is anything special we would like to thank Jesus for, now is the time to say it.

6. Hail Holy Queen

Father: Jesus is our King, Mary, His Mother is our Queen. Many Catholics, by their deeds, their bad talk, their immodesty, offend the Immaculate Heart of our Queen. Let us make up for this and at the same time promise our Mother that we will try not to offend her.

Hail Holy Queen, our life, our sweetness and our hope. To thee do we cry, poor banished children of Eve; to thee do we send up our cries, mourning and weeping in this valley of tears. Turn then, most gracious advocate, thine eyes of mercy toward us, and after this exile, show us the fruit of thy womb, Jesus. O Clement, O Loving, O Sweet Virgin Mary! Pray for us, O Holy Mother of God, that we may be made worthy of the promises of Christ.

7. All sign the Enthronement "Covenant" (certificate), first, the father, then mother and then the children. It is to be framed and hung near the Enthronement shrine.

8. Final Hymn

"HEART OF JESUS, KING AND SAVIOR"
(Melody: Tantum Ergo—do-re-mi-do)

> Heart of Jesus, King and Savior
> Hear our prayer—Thy Kingdom come!
> In our family, school and parish
> Be our friend, our King of love.
> Through Your Eucharistic Banquet
> Make our hearts unite as one.
>
> God the Father, our Creator,
> Loved us so, He gave His Son.
> See the Crib, the Cross, the altar,
> Proofs of love for everyone.
> Heart of Jesus, send Your Spirit—
> Love's repaid by love alone.
>
> Heart of Jesus, King and Brother,
> In our homes set up Your throne.
> Share our every joy and sorrow
> You we love and You alone.
> Help us truly love our neighbor,
> Make love reign in heart and home!

9. The parents now give their children the parental blessing. The children kneel before the parents. First the father, then the mother, make the sign of the Cross on the forehead of each child saying: "I bless you, my child, in the Name of the Father and of the Son, and of the Holy Spirit." The child answers, Amen.

10. In honor of the Divine Guest, refreshments will now be served.

Section Three

DAILY PRAYERS

The Mystical Mass Prayer—by Luke B. Zimmer, SS.CC.

Saint Michael, the Archangel, defend us in battle, be our safeguard against the wickedness and snares of the devil. May God rebuke him we humbly pray; and do you, Prince of the heavenly host, by the power of God, cast into hell Satan and all the evil spirits, who wander through the world seeking the ruin of souls.

Most Sacred Heart of Jesus, have mercy on us (three times). I wish to invite each angel and saint in heaven and soul in purgatory to pray with me and for me.

Eternal Father, I offer to You through the Immaculate and Sorrowful Heart of Mary, in the Holy Spirit, the Body, Blood, Soul and Divinity of Your Divine Son, Jesus Christ, from all the altars throughout the world at each Holy Mass which is celebrated on this day and every day until the end of time.

To each Mass, I wish to unite everything that took place in the lives of Jesus, Mary, and Joseph while they lived on earth (think of the things in detail or in general) and their existence in heaven for all eternity.

I wish to unite everything which took place in the life of each angel in heaven (creation, trial, victory, glory, and joy in heaven, the honor and glory given to God).

I wish to unite all that took place in the life of each of the Saints in Heaven while they were living on earth, after death, and the glory they give to You in Heaven (offer all their prayers, sufferings, trials, successes, failures and faults).

I wish to unite everything good in the life of each person in purgatory, and the happiness they will enjoy in heaven, and the honor and glory they will give to You.

I wish to unite every good thought, word, and deed in the

life of each person who is living and will live until the end of time.

I wish to unite the honor and glory of all creation.

Finally, I wish to unite myself with Christ in each Mass which I offer to You. Take me and do with me what You wish, when You wish, and as long as You wish. Give me the serenity to accept the things I cannot change, the courage to change the things I can, and the wisdom to know the difference.

Help me to love You, my God, with my whole heart and soul, with all my strength and mind and my neighbor as myself for the love of You.

I wish to accept the type of death You wish me to die—when, where, how and why.

I offer all through Him, with Him, in Him, in the unity of the Holy Spirit for Your glory and honor, Almighty Father, forever and ever.

Let each Holy Mass be an act of love and adoration which I wish to offer to You, God the Father, since You are our God, our Creator, and our Father. To You, God the Son, since You are our God, our Redeemer, Mediator, King, Judge, and Brother. To You, God the Holy Spirit, since You are our God, our Advocate, our Paraclete, our Sanctifier.

Let each Holy Mass be an act of thanksgiving for all the gifts and graces given to each person and each one who will exist, especially for . . . .

Let each Holy Mass be an act of reparation for all the sins that have, are, and will be committed until the end of the world. Especially sins of ingratitude, indifference, unbelief, swearing, cursing, blasphemy, sacrilege, anger, hatred, murder, and all sins of impurity; especially for my sins of . . . .

From each Holy Mass, O Triune God, I ask You to bless my father, mother, sisters, brothers, relatives, friends, and especially . . . .

Bless the Holy Father, the Pope, the cardinals, bishops, priests, sisters, brothers, and all those aspiring to serve You in religious life, especially . . . and may more and more aspire to God's service.

Bless the poor, the sick, the dying, and the poor souls in Purgatory.

Bless and cure ....

Let each Holy Mass be a petition for peace, and for an increase of faith, hope and love.

Cum Permissu:
        Harold K. Meyer, SS.CC.
        Provincial of Hawaii
Nihil Obstat:
    John B. Reed
    Censor Librorum
Imprimatur:
    John J. Scanlan, D.D
    Bishop of Honolulu
December 8, 1968

Chaplet of the Holy Spirit
Homage of Adoration to the Paraclete
in Honor of His Seven Gifts

Since this is the age of the Holy Spirit, here is a practical suggestion of a simple, yet beautiful, way of honoring the Holy Spirit and drawing His sevenfold gifts upon us.

Let us endeavor to instill, in the first place, love of the Paraclete, as a strong and doctrinal devotion suitable to the choicest among pious souls.

Let us, therefore, form the praiseworthy habit of reciting the Chaplet which is proposed here, as a homage to the Holy Spirit.

Come, Holy Spirit, enlighten my mind! Come, inflame my heart!

1. Take your beads (the Blessed Virgin's rosary) and recite the Apostles' Creed.

2. After the Creed, very slowly and devoutly, the Glory be to the Father.

3. Then say the Our Father.

4. Now, very fervently, say this ejaculation: "Father, send us the promised Paraclete, through Jesus Christ our Lord. Amen."

5. Now on each bead, instead of the Hail Mary say with a burning heart: "Come, Holy Spirit, fill the hearts of Your faithful and kindle in them the fire of Your love!"

6. After the tenth bead recite the following official prayer: "Send forth Your Spirit and they shall be created, and You shall renew the face of the earth.

O God, who did instruct the hearts of the faithful by the light of the Holy Spirit, grant us by the same Spirit to be truly wise and evermore to rejoice in His consolations. Through Christ our Lord. Amen.

7. Then recite the second decade and all the others in the same way as explained (beginning at 3): "Our Father ..."

8. After the seventh and last decade, recite the "Hail, Holy Queen" in honor of the Blessed Virgin, our Heavenly Queen, who presided in the Cenacle on the great Sunday of Pentecost.

A few short reflections may be made on seven glorious mysteries relating to seven wonderful operations of the Paraclete.

These meditations should be made briefly, between every ten beads.

1st Mystery: Let us honor the Holy Spirit and adore Him who is love substantial, proceeding from the Father and the Son, and uniting Them in an infinite and eternal charity.

2nd Mystery: Let us honor the operation of the Holy Spirit and adore Him in the Immaculate Conception of Mary, sanctifying her, from the first moment, with the plentitude of grace.

3rd Mystery: Let us honor the operation of the Holy Spirit and adore Him in the Incarnation of the Word, the Son of God by His Divine Nature, and the Son of the Virgin by the flesh.

4th Mystery: Let us honor the operation of the Holy Spirit and adore Him giving birth to the Church on the glorious day of Pentecost in the Cenacle.

5th Mystery: Let us honor the operation of the Holy Spirit and adore Him dwelling in the Church and assisting Her faithfully according to the Divine promise, even to the consummation of the world.

6th Mystery: Let us honor the wonderful operation of the Holy Spirit creating within the Church that other Christ, the Priest, and conferring the plentitude of the priesthood on the Bishops.

7th Mystery: Let us honor the operation of the Holy Spirit and adore Him in the heroic virtue of the saints in the Church, that hidden and marvelous work of the "Adorable Sanctifier."

Practices:

Recite the Chaplet of the Holy Spirit often, even daily. Recite it:

1. Especially on Sundays.

2. When some important decision must be made; at certain grave moments and when special spiritual help is needed.

3. As a preparation for the Feast of Pentecost; this day witnessed the Birth of the Church of Christ.

4. Every day during recollections and retreats.

Written by Father Mateo, SS.CC.
Imprimatur:
Carolus Hubertus Le Blond
Bishop of St. Joseph

The Rosary

Monday and Thursday:
Joyful Mysteries
1. Annunciation
2. Visitation
3. Nativity
4. Presentation
5. Finding of Jesus in the temple

Tuesday and Friday:
Sorrowful Mysteries
1. Agony in the Garden
2. Scourging
3. Crowning with Thorns
4. Carrying of the Cross
5. Crucifixion

Sunday, Wednesday, and Saturday:
Glorious Mysteries
1. Resurrection
2. Ascension
3. Descent of the Holy Spirit
4. Assumption of the Blessed Virgin Mary
5. Crowning of the Blessed Virgin Mary in heaven

Renewal of Total Commitment to Jesus through Mary

In the presence of all the heavenly court, I, N. . . . , choose you today as my Mother, I deliver and consecrate myself to you completely; my body and soul, my goods, both interior and exterior, and even the value of all my good actions, past, present, and future.

I also renew and ratify today in your hands, O Immaculate Mother, the vows of my baptism; I renounce forever Satan, his pomps and works.

Through your hands, O Blessed Mother, I consecrate and commit myself entirely to Jesus Christ, your Son and my Brother, to carry my cross after Him all the days of my life, and to be more faithful to Him than ever before.

Grant that I may be faithful in living this commitment every day of my life. Amen.

Renewal Prayer of the Consecration of the Family to the Immaculate Heart

Queen of the most holy Rosary, and tender Mother of men,/ to fulfill the desires of the Sacred Heart,/ and the request of the Vicar of your Son on earth,/ we renew our consecration to you, and to your Immaculate Heart,/ and to recommend to you,/ all the families of our nation and of the world.

Please accept our consecration, dearest Mother,/ and use us and all families as you wish,/ to accomplish your designs upon the world.

O Immaculate Heart of Mary,/ Queen of heaven and earth, and of our family,/ rule over us, together with the Sacred Heart of Jesus Christ, our King,/ Save us from the spreading flood of modern paganism, kindle in our hearts and homes the love of purity,/ and the practice of the Christian life,/ and an ardent zeal for souls, and for the holiness of family life.

We come with confidence to you,/ O Throne of Grace and Mother of Fair love;/ inflame us with the same Divine fire/ which has inflamed your own Immaculate Heart.

Make our hearts and homes your shrine,/ and through us make

the Heart of Jesus/ rule and triumph in every family in the world. Amen.

Renewal Prayer of the Enthronement of the Sacred Heart of Jesus

Most kind Jesus, humbly kneeling at Thy feet,/ we renew the consecration of our family to Thy Divine Heart.

Be thou our King forever./ In Thee we have full and entire confidence./ May Thy Spirit penetrate our thoughts,/ our desires, our words and our deeds./ Bless our undertakings,/ share in our joys, in our trials,/ in our labors.

Grant us to know Thee better,/ to love Thee more,/ to serve Thee without faltering.

By the Immaculate Heart of Mary, Queen of Peace,/ set up Thy Kingdom in our country./ Enter closely into the midst of our families and make them Thine own/ through the solemn Enthronement of Thy Sacred Heart,/ so that soon one cry may resound from home to home:/ May the triumphant Heart of Jesus be everywhere loved,/ blessed, and glorified forever./ To the Sacred Hearts of Jesus and Mary/ be honor and glory forever and ever.

Sacred Heart of Jesus, protect our families.

Section Four

CATALOG OF RELIGIOUS BOOKS, BOOKLETS, ARTICLES

1. E—rec LP Record on Enthronement $4.00

2. E-Film "The Sacred Heart Enthroned"
   Enthronement Film   Rental 10.00
                                          Purchase 100.00

3. SH Bad Badge of the Sacred Hearts .... .10

4. Companion Pictures (Laminated) 9.00
   SH-3 Sacred Heart 13-1/2 x 16 1/2
   IHM-3 Immaculate Heart 13-1/2 x 16-1/2

5. SH-2 Sacred Heart, Jesus King of Love
   10-1/2 x 13-1/2 .... 1.50

6. IHM-2 Immaculate Heart 10-1/2 x 13-1/2 .... 1.50

7. Fire "The Firebrand" Biography of Father Mateo
   by Father Francis Larkin, SS.CC. 4.00

8. Mass-En L .... .05
   Mass-EN 11 Enthronement Mass Missalette

9. Little Chaplet of the Holy Spirit .... .05

10. Family Prayer Renewal in the Heart of Christ
    (15 prayer formulas) Blue booklet .... .20
    (Scriptural Enthronement Ritual) Green booklet .... .25

11. Official MSH Lapel Pin 1.00

12. Jesus, King of Love, By Father Mateo, SS.CC 2.00

13. Enthronement of the Sacred Heart, Fr. Larkin, SS.CC. ... 2.00

14. Kit-Fd-4 copies of Cerem 1.50

15. NA-Night Adoration
    MHWJ-My Hour with Jesus
    HH—R Holy Hour-Religious
    HH-RC-Holy Hour-Religious Communities
    NA-RN-Holy Hour-Nurses
    NA-Col-Holy Hour-College Students
    FHH-Family Holy Hour .... Ea. .25

    National Enthronement Center
    3 Adams Street
    Fairhaven, Mass. 02719

The Imitation of Christ, by Thomas a Kempis .... .85
    Image Books
    A Division of Doubleday & Company, Inc.
    Garden City, N.Y.

7-Color Lithograph of the Sacred Heart .... .05
    Size 7-1/2 x 12-1/2
    Order in lots of 50 or more
    Messenger Corporation
    Auburn, Indiana 46706

Color Portraits of the Sacred Heart 3/1.00
    Size 8x10   10/2.00
    The Woeber Family
    Box 45441 (A)
    Dallas, Texas 75235

Prayer for a Holy Hour .... .10
    Benedictine Convent of Perpetual Adoration
    Clyde, Missouri 64432

Outlines of the 16 Documents of Vatican II .... .65
   The Long Island Catholic
   53 North Park Avenue
   Rockville Center, N.Y. 11570

"Renewal in the Heart of Christ" .... .50
   Special Sacred Heart Issue   (10 or more)   .40
   of Immaculata Magazine   (100 or more)   .30
   Immaculata .... $5.00 a year
   Marytown Press
   8000-39th Ave.
   Kenosha, Wisconsin 53141

The Pope Speaks .... $8.00 per year
   3622 12th Street NE
   Washington, D.C. 20017

The Documents of Vatican II 2.25
   by Walter M. Abbott, S.J.
   Borromeo Guild
   1530 W. 9th St
   Los Angeles, Calif. 90015

The Apostolate of Christian Renewal Booklet 1.50
Apostolic Renewal 3.95
The Family Home Missions 4.95
   By Father Luke Zimmer, SS.CC.
   Apostolate of Christian Renewal
   3 St. James Park
   Los Angeles, Calif. 90007